PENGUIN BOOKS

Hiroshima

John Hersey was born in Tientsin, China, in 1914, and lived there until 1925, when his family returned to the United States. He studied at Yale and Clare College, Cambridge, served for a time as Sinclair Lewis's secretary, and then worked for several years as a journalist. He published seventeen works of fiction, including the Pulitzer Prize winning *A Bell for Adano* (1945), *The Wall* (1950), *A Single Pebble* (1956), *The Child Buyer* (1960), *The Call* (1985), *Fling and Other Stories* (1990) and *Antonietta* (1991). Besides *Hiroshima*, which was first published in 1946, he wrote six books of essays and reportage. From 1965 to 1970 John Hersey was Master of Pierson College at Yale, and he taught at the University until 1984. He was a President of the Author's League of America and Chancellor of the American Academy of Arts and Letters. John Hersey died in 1993.

John Hersey

HIROSHIMA

PENGUIN BOOKS

PENGUIN BOOKS

Published by the Penguin Group
Penguin Books Ltd, 80 Strand, London WC2R 0RL, England
Penguin Putnam Inc., 375 Hudson Street, New York, New York 10014, USA
Penguin Books Australia Ltd, 250 Camberwell Road, Camberwell, Victoria 3124, Australia
Penguin Books Canada Ltd, 10 Alcorn Avenue, Toronto, Ontario, Canada M4V 3B2
Penguin Books India (P) Ltd, 11 Community Centre, Panchsheel Park, New Delhi – 110 017, India
Penguin Books (NZ) Ltd, Cnr Rosedale and Airborne Roads, Albany, Auckland, New Zealand
Penguin Books (South Africa) (Pty) Ltd, 24 Sturdee Avenue, Rosebank 2196, South Africa

Penguin Books Ltd, Registered Offices: 80 Strand, London WC2R 0RL, England

www.penguin.com

First published in the *New Yorker*, August 1946
Published in Penguin Books 1946
Reissued as a Penguin Special 1958
Republished by Hamish Hamilton 1966
Reissued in Penguin Books 1972
This edition, with a new chapter, first published by Alfred A. Knopf, Inc. 1985
Published in Penguin Books 1986
Reprinted in Penguin Classics 2001

2

Printed in England by Clays Ltd, St Ives plc

Contents

Hiroshima

I · *A Noiseless Flash*

At exactly fifteen minutes past eight in the morning, on August 6, 1945, Japanese time, at the moment when the atomic bomb flashed above Hiroshima, Miss Toshiko Sasaki, a clerk in the personnel department of the East Asia Tin Works, had just sat down at her place in the plant office and was turning her head to speak to the girl at the next desk. At that same moment, Dr. Masakazu Fujii was settling down cross-legged to read the Osaka *Asahi* on the porch of his private hospital, overhanging one of the seven deltaic rivers which divide Hiroshima; Mrs. Hatsuyo Nakamura, a tailor's widow, stood by the window of her kitchen, watching a neighbor tearing down his house because it lay in the path of an air-raid-defense fire lane; Father Wilhelm Kleinsorge, a German priest of the Society of Jesus, reclined in his underwear on a cot on the top floor of his order's three-story mission house, reading a Jesuit magazine, *Stimmen der Zeit;* Dr. Terufumi Sasaki, a young member of the surgical staff of the city's large, modern Red Cross Hospital, walked along one of the hospital corridors with a blood specimen for a Wassermann test in his hand; and the Reverend Mr. Kiyoshi Tanimoto, pastor of the Hiroshima Methodist Church, paused at the door of a rich man's house in Koi, the city's western suburb, and prepared to unload a handcart full of things he had evacuated from town in fear of the massive B-29 raid which everyone expected Hiroshima to suffer. A hundred thousand people were killed by the atomic bomb, and these six were among the survivors. They still wonder why they lived when so many others died. Each of them counts many small items of chance or volition —a step taken in time, a decision to go indoors, catching one streetcar instead of the next—that spared him. And now each knows that in the act of survival he lived a dozen lives and saw more death than he ever thought he would see. At the time, none of them knew anything.

THE Reverend Mr. Tanimoto got up at five o'clock that morning. He was alone in the parsonage, because for some time his wife had been commuting with their year-old baby to spend nights with a friend in Ushida, a suburb to the north. Of all the important cities of Japan, only two, Kyoto and Hiroshima, had not been visited in strength by *B-san,* or Mr. B, as the Japanese, with a mixture of respect and unhappy familiarity, called the B-29; and Mr. Tanimoto, like all his neighbors and friends, was almost sick with anxiety. He had heard uncomfortably detailed accounts of mass raids on Kure, Iwakuni, Tokuyama, and other nearby towns; he was sure Hiroshima's turn would come soon. He had slept badly the night before, because there had been several air-raid warnings. Hiroshima had been getting such warnings almost every night for weeks, for at that time the B-29s were using Lake Biwa, northeast of Hiroshima, as a rendezvous point, and no matter what city the Americans planned to hit, the Superfortresses streamed in over the coast near Hiroshima. The frequency of the warnings and the continued abstinence of Mr. B with respect to Hiroshima had made its citizens jittery; a rumor was going around that the Americans were saving something special for the city.

Mr. Tanimoto was a small man, quick to talk, laugh, and cry. He wore his black hair parted in the middle and rather long; the prominence of the frontal bones just above his eyebrows and the smallness of his mustache, mouth, and chin gave him a strange, old-young look, boyish and yet wise, weak and yet fiery. He moved nervously and fast, but with a restraint which suggested that he was a cautious, thoughtful man. He showed, indeed, just those qualities in the uneasy days before the bomb fell. Besides having his wife spend the nights in Ushida, Mr. Tanimoto had been carrying all the portable things from his church, in the close-packed residential district called Nagaragawa, to a house that belonged to a rayon manufacturer in Koi, two miles from the center of town. The rayon man, a Mr. Matsui, had opened his then unoccupied estate to a large number of his friends and acquaintances, so that they might evacuate whatever they wished to a safe distance from the probable target area. Mr. Tanimoto had had no difficulty in moving chairs, hymnals, Bibles, altar gear, and church records by pushcart himself, but the organ console and an upright piano required some aid. A friend of his named Matsuo had, the day before, helped him get the piano out to Koi; in return, he had promised this day to assist Mr. Matsuo in hauling out a daughter's belongings. That is why he had risen so early.

Mr. Tanimoto cooked his own breakfast. He felt awfully tired. The effort of moving the piano the day before, a sleepless night, weeks of worry and unbalanced diet, the cares of his parish—all combined to make him feel hardly adequate to the new day's work. There was another thing, too: Mr. Tanimoto had studied theology at Emory College, in Atlanta, Georgia; he had graduated in 1940; he spoke excellent English; he dressed in American clothes; he had corresponded with many American friends right up to the time the war began; and among a people obsessed with a fear of being spied upon—perhaps almost obsessed himself—he found himself growing increasingly uneasy. The police had questioned him several times, and just a few days before, he had heard that an influential acquaintance, a Mr. Tanaka, a retired officer of the Toyo Kisen Kaisha steamship line, an anti-Christian, a man famous in Hiroshima for his showy philanthropies and notorious for his personal tyrannies, had been telling people that Tanimoto should not be trusted. In compensation, to show himself publicly a good Japanese, Mr. Tanimoto had taken on the chairmanship of his local *tonarigumi*, or Neighborhood Association, and to his other duties and concerns this position had added the business of organizing air-raid defense for about twenty families.

Before six o'clock that morning, Mr. Tanimoto started for Mr. Matsuo's house. There he found that their burden was to be a *tansu*, a large Japanese cabinet, full of clothing and household goods. The two men set out. The morning was perfectly clear and so warm that the day promised to be uncomfortable. A few minutes after they started, the air-raid siren went off—a minute-long blast that warned of approaching planes but indicated to the people of Hiroshima only a slight degree of danger, since it sounded every morning at this time, when an American weather plane came over. The two men pulled and pushed the handcart through the city streets. Hiroshima was a fan-shaped city, lying mostly on the six islands formed by the seven estuarial rivers that branch out from the Ota River; its main commercial and residential districts, covering about four square miles in the center of the city, contained three-quarters of its population, which had been reduced by several evacuation programs from a wartime peak of 380,000 to about 245,000. Factories and other

7

residential districts, or suburbs, lay compactly around the edges of the city. To the south were the docks, an airport, and the island-studded Inland Sea. A rim of mountains runs around the other three sides of the delta. Mr. Tanimoto and Mr. Matsuo took their way through the shopping center, already full of people, and across two of the rivers to the sloping streets of Koi, and up them to the outskirts and foothills. As they started up a valley away from the tight-ranked houses, the all-clear sounded. (The Japanese radar operators, detecting only three planes, supposed that they comprised a reconnaissance.) Pushing the handcart up to the rayon man's house was tiring, and the men, after they had maneuvered their load into the driveway and to the front steps, paused to rest awhile. They stood with a wing of the house between them and the city. Like most homes in this part of Japan, the house consisted of a wooden frame and wooden walls supporting a heavy tile roof. Its front hall, packed with rolls of bedding and clothing, looked like a cool cave full of fat cushions. Opposite the house, to the right of the front door, there was a large, finicky rock garden. There was no sound of planes. The morning was still; the place was cool and pleasant.

Then a tremendous flash of light cut across the sky. Mr. Tanimoto has a distinct recollection that it travelled from east to west, from the city toward the hills. It seemed a sheet of sun. Both he and Mr. Matsuo reacted in terror—and both had time to react (for they were 3,500 yards, or two miles, from the center of the explosion). Mr. Matsuo dashed up the front steps into the house and dived among the bedrolls and buried himself there. Mr. Tanimoto took four or five steps and threw himself between two big rocks in the garden. He bellied up very hard against one of them. As his face was against the stone, he did not see what happened. He felt a sudden pressure, and then splinters and pieces of board and fragments of tile fell on him. He heard no roar. (Almost no one in Hiroshima recalls hearing any noise of the bomb. But a fisherman in his sampan on the Inland Sea near Tsuzu, the man with whom Mr. Tanimoto's mother-in-law and sister-in-law were living, saw the flash and heard a tremendous explosion; he was nearly twenty miles from Hiroshima, but the thunder was greater than when the B-29s hit Iwakuni, only five miles away.)

When he dared, Mr. Tanimoto raised his head and saw that the rayon man's house had collapsed. He thought a bomb had fallen directly on it. Such clouds of dust had risen that there was a sort of twilight around. In panic, not thinking for the moment of Mr. Matsuo under the ruins, he dashed out into the street. He noticed as he ran that the concrete wall of the estate had fallen over—toward the house rather than away from it. In the street, the first thing he saw was a squad of soldiers who had been burrowing into the hillside opposite, making one of the thousands of dugouts in which the Japanese apparently intended to resist invasion, hill by hill, life for life; the soldiers were coming out of the hole, where they should have been safe,

and blood was running from their heads, chests, and
backs. They were silent and dazed.

Under what seemed to be a local dust cloud, the
day grew darker and darker.

At nearly midnight, the night before the bomb was
dropped, an announcer on the city's radio station said
that about two hundred B-29s were approaching south-
ern Honshu and advised the population of Hiroshima
to evacuate to their designated "safe areas." Mrs. Hatsuyo Nakamura, the tailor's widow, who lived in the
section called Nobori-cho and who had long had a habit
of doing as she was told, got her three children—a ten-
year-old boy, Toshio, an eight-year-old girl, Yaeko, and
a five-year-old girl, Myeko—out of bed and dressed
them and walked with them to the military area known
as the East Parade Ground, on the northeast edge of the
city. There she unrolled some mats and the children lay
down on them. They slept until about two, when they
were awakened by the roar of the planes going over
Hiroshima.

As soon as the planes had passed, Mrs. Nakamura
started back with her children. They reached home a
little after two-thirty and she immediately turned on
the radio, which, to her distress, was just then broad-
casting a fresh warning. When she looked at the children and saw how tired they were, and when she
thought of the number of trips they had made in past
weeks, all to no purpose, to the East Parade Ground,
she decided that in spite of the instructions on the

radio, she simply could not face starting out all over again. She put the children in their bedrolls on the floor, lay down herself at three o'clock, and fell asleep at once, so soundly that when planes passed over later, she did not waken to their sound.

The siren jarred her awake at about seven. She arose, dressed quickly, and hurried to the house of Mr. Nakamoto, the head of her Neighborhood Association, and asked him what she should do. He said that she should remain at home unless an urgent warning—a series of intermittent blasts of the siren—was sounded. She returned home, lit the stove in the kitchen, set some rice to cook, and sat down to read that morning's Hiroshima *Chugoku*. To her relief, the all-clear sounded at eight o'clock. She heard the children stirring, so she went and gave each of them a handful of peanuts and told them to stay on their bedrolls, because they were tired from the night's walk. She had hoped that they would go back to sleep, but the man in the house directly to the south began to make a terrible hullabaloo of hammering, wedging, ripping, and splitting. The prefectural government, convinced, as everyone in Hiroshima was, that the city would be attacked soon, had begun to press with threats and warnings for the completion of wide fire lanes, which, it was hoped, might act in conjunction with the rivers to localize any fires started by an incendiary raid; and the neighbor was reluctantly sacrificing his home to the city's safety. Just the day before, the prefecture had ordered all able-bodied girls from the secondary schools to spend a few days helping to clear these lanes, and they started work soon after the all-clear sounded.

Mrs. Nakamura went back to the kitchen, looked at the rice, and began watching the man next door. At first, she was annoyed with him for making so much noise, but then she was moved almost to tears by pity. Her emotion was specifically directed toward her neighbor, tearing down his home, board by board, at a time when there was so much unavoidable destruction, but undoubtedly she also felt a generalized, community pity, to say nothing of self-pity. She had not had an easy time. Her husband, Isawa, had gone into the Army just after Myeko was born, and she had heard nothing from or of him for a long time, until, on March 5, 1942, she received a seven-word telegram: "Isawa died an honorable death at Singapore." She learned later that he had died on February 15th, the day Singapore fell, and that he had been a corporal. Isawa had been a not particularly prosperous tailor, and his only capital was a Sankoku sewing machine. After his death, when his allotments stopped coming, Mrs. Nakamura got out the machine and began to take in piecework herself, and since then had supported the children, but poorly, by sewing.

As Mrs. Nakamura stood watching her neighbor, everything flashed whiter than any white she had ever seen. She did not notice what happened to the man next door; the reflex of a mother set her in motion toward her children. She had taken a single step (the house was 1,350 yards, or three-quarters of a mile, from the center of the explosion) when something picked her up and she seemed to fly into the next room over the raised sleeping platform, pursued by parts of her house.

Timbers fell around her as she landed, and a shower of tiles pommelled her; everything became dark, for she was buried. The debris did not cover her deeply. She rose up and freed herself. She heard a child cry, "Mother, help me!," and saw her youngest—Myeko, the five-year-old—buried up to her breast and unable to move. As Mrs. Nakamura started frantically to claw her way toward the baby, she could see or hear nothing of her other children.

IN THE DAYS right before the bombing, Dr. Masakazu Fujii, being prosperous, hedonistic, and at the time not too busy, had been allowing himself the luxury of sleeping until nine or nine-thirty, but fortunately he had to get up early the morning the bomb was dropped to see a house guest off on a train. He rose at six, and half an hour later walked with his friend to the station, not far away, across two of the rivers. He was back home by seven, just as the siren sounded its sustained warning. He ate breakfast and then, because the morning was already hot, undressed down to his underwear and went out on the porch to read the paper. This porch —in fact, the whole building—was curiously constructed. Dr. Fujii was the proprietor of a peculiarly Japanese institution: a private, single-doctor hospital. This building, perched beside and over the water of the Kyo River, and next to the bridge of the same name, contained thirty rooms for thirty patients and their kinfolk—for, according to Japanese custom, when a person falls sick and goes to a hospital, one or more members of his family go and live there with him, to cook for him, bathe, massage, and read to him, and to offer incessant familial sympathy, without which a Japanese patient would be miserable indeed. Dr. Fujii had no beds—only straw mats—for his patients. He did, however, have all sorts of modern equipment: an X-ray machine, diathermy apparatus, and a fine tiled laboratory. The structure rested two-thirds on the land, one-third on piles over the tidal waters of the Kyo. This overhang, the part of the building where Dr. Fujii lived, was queer-looking, but it was cool in summer and from the porch, which faced away from the center of the city, the prospect of the river, with pleasure boats drifting up and down it, was always refreshing. Dr. Fujii had occasionally had anxious moments when the Ota and its mouth branches rose to flood, but the piling was apparently firm enough and the house had always held.

Dr. Fujii had been relatively idle for about a month because in July, as the number of untouched cities in Japan dwindled and as Hiroshima seemed more and more inevitably a target, he began turning patients away, on the ground that in case of a fire raid he would not be able to evacuate them. Now he had only two patients left—a woman from Yano, injured in the shoulder, and a young man of twenty-five recovering from burns he had suffered when the steel factory near

1 4

A Noiseless Flash

Hiroshima in which he worked had been hit. Dr. Fujii had six nurses to tend his patients. His wife and children were safe; his wife and one son were living outside Osaka, and another son and two daughters were in the country on Kyushu. A niece was living with him, and a maid and a manservant. He had little to do and did not mind, for he had saved some money. At fifty, he was healthy, convivial, and calm, and he was pleased to pass the evenings drinking whiskey with friends, always sensibly and for the sake of conversation. Before the war, he had affected brands imported from Scotland and America; now he was perfectly satisfied with the best Japanese brand, Suntory.

Dr. Fujii sat down cross-legged in his underwear on the spotless matting of the porch, put on his glasses, and started reading the Osaka *Asahi*. He liked to read the Osaka news because his wife was there. He saw the flash. To him—faced away from the center and looking at his paper—it seemed a brilliant yellow. Startled, he began to rise to his feet. In that moment (he was 1,550 yards from the center), the hospital leaned behind his rising and, with a terrible ripping noise, toppled into the river. The Doctor, still in the act of getting to his feet, was thrown forward and around and over; he was buffeted and gripped; he lost track of everything, because things were so speeded up; he felt the water.

Dr. Fujii hardly had time to think that he was dying before he realized that he was alive, squeezed tightly by two long timbers in a V across his chest, like a morsel suspended between two huge chopsticks—held upright, so that he could not move, with his head miraculously above water and his torso and legs in it. The remains of his hospital were all around him in a mad assortment of splintered lumber and materials for the relief of pain. His left shoulder hurt terribly. His glasses were gone.

FATHER WILHELM KLEINSORGE, of the Society of Jesus, was, on the morning of the explosion, in rather frail condition. The Japanese wartime diet had not sustained him, and he felt the strain of being a foreigner in an increasingly xenophobic Japan; even a German, since the defeat of the Fatherland, was unpopular. Father Kleinsorge had, at thirty-eight, the look of a boy growing too fast—thin in the face, with a prominent Adam's apple, a hollow chest, dangling hands, big feet. He walked clumsily, leaning forward a little. He was tired all the time. To make matters worse, he had suffered for two days, along with Father Cieslik, a fellow-priest, from a rather painful and urgent diarrhea, which they blamed on the beans and black ration bread they were obliged to eat. Two other priests then living in the mission compound, which was in the Nobori-cho section—Father Superior LaSalle and Father Schiffer—had happily escaped this affliction.

Father Kleinsorge woke up about six the morning the bomb was dropped, and half an hour later—he was a bit tardy because of his sickness—he began to read Mass in the mission chapel, a small Japanese-style wooden building which was without pews, since its worshippers knelt on the usual Japanese matted floor, facing an altar graced with splendid silks, brass, silver, and heavy embroideries. This morning, a Monday, the only worshippers were Mr. Takemoto, a theological student living in the mission house; Mr. Fukai, the secretary of the diocese; Mrs. Murata, the mission's devoutly Christian housekeeper; and his fellow-priests. After Mass, while Father Kleinsorge was reading the Prayers of Thanksgiving, the siren sounded. He stopped the service and the missionaries retired across the compound to the bigger building. There, in his room on the ground floor, to the right of the front door, Father Kleinsorge changed into a military uniform which he had acquired when he was teaching at the Rokko Middle School in Kobe and which he wore during air-raid alerts.

After an alarm, Father Kleinsorge always went out and scanned the sky, and in this instance, when he stepped outside, he was glad to see only the single weather plane that flew over Hiroshima each day about this time. Satisfied that nothing would happen, he went in and breakfasted with the other Fathers on substitute coffee and ration bread, which, under the circumstances, was especially repugnant to him. The Fathers sat and talked awhile, until, at eight, they heard the all-clear. They went then to various parts of the building. Father Schiffer retired to his room to do some writing. Father Cieslik sat in his room in a straight chair with a pillow over his stomach to ease his pain, and read. Father Superior LaSalle stood at the window of his room, thinking. Father Kleinsorge went up to a room on the third floor, took off all his clothes except his underwear, and stretched out on his right side on a cot and began reading his *Stimmen der Zeit*.

After the terrible flash—which, Father Kleinsorge later realized, reminded him of something he had read as a boy about a large meteor colliding with the earth —he had time (since he was 1,400 yards from the center) for one thought: A bomb has fallen directly on us. Then, for a few seconds or minutes, he went out of his mind.

Father Kleinsorge never knew how he got out of the house. The next things he was conscious of were that he was wandering around in the mission's vegetable garden in his underwear, bleeding slightly from small cuts along his left flank; that all the buildings round about had fallen down except the Jesuits' mission house, which had long before been braced and double-braced by a priest named Gropper, who was terrified of earthquakes; that the day had turned dark; and that Murata-*san*, the housekeeper, was nearby, crying over and over, "*Shu Jesusu, awaremi tamai!* Our Lord Jesus, have pity on us!"

ON THE TRAIN on the way into Hiroshima from the country, where he lived with his mother, Dr. Terufumi Sasaki, the Red Cross Hospital surgeon, thought over an unpleasant nightmare he had had the night before. His mother's home was in Mukaihara, thirty miles from the city, and it took him two hours by train and tram to reach the hospital. He had slept uneasily all night and had wakened an hour earlier than usual, and, feeling sluggish and slightly feverish, had debated whether to go to the hospital at all; his sense of duty finally forced him to go, and he had started out on an earlier train than he took most mornings. The dream had particularly frightened him because it was so closely associated, on the surface at least, with a disturbing actuality. He was only twenty-five years old and had just completed his training at the Eastern Medical University, in Tsingtao, China. He was something of an idealist and was much distressed by the inadequacy of medical facilities in the country town where his mother lived. Quite on his own, and without a permit, he had begun visiting a few sick people out there in the evenings, after his eight hours at the hospital and four hours' commuting. He had recently learned that the penalty for practicing without a permit was severe; a fellow-doctor whom he had asked about it had given him a serious scolding. Nevertheless, he had continued to practice. In his dream, he had been at the bedside of a country patient when the police and the doctor he had consulted burst into the room, seized him, dragged him outside, and beat him up cruelly. On the train, he just about decided to give up the work in Mukaihara, since he felt it would be impossible to get a permit, because the authorities would hold that it would conflict with his duties at the Red Cross Hospital.

At the terminus, he caught a streetcar at once. (He

later calculated that if he had taken his customary train that morning, and if he had had to wait a few minutes for the streetcar, as often happened, he would have been close to the center at the time of the explosion and would surely have perished.) He arrived at the hospital at seven-forty and reported to the chief surgeon. A few minutes later, he went to a room on the first floor and drew blood from the arm of a man in order to perform a Wassermann test. The laboratory containing the incubators for the test was on the third floor. With the blood specimen in his left hand, walking in a kind of distraction he had felt all morning, probably because of the dream and his restless night, he started along the main corridor on his way toward the stairs. He was one step beyond an open window when the light of the bomb was reflected, like a gigantic photographic flash, in the corridor. He ducked down on one knee and said to himself, as only a Japanese would, "Sasaki, *gambare!* Be brave!" Just then (the building was 1,650 yards from the center), the blast ripped through the hospital. The glasses he was wearing flew off his face; the bottle of blood crashed against one wall; his Japanese slippers zipped out from under his feet—but otherwise, thanks to where he stood, he was untouched.

Dr. Sasaki shouted the name of the chief surgeon and rushed around to the man's office and found him terribly cut by glass. The hospital was in horrible confusion: heavy partitions and ceilings had fallen on patients, beds had overturned, windows had blown in and cut people, blood was spattered on the walls and floors, instruments were everywhere, many of the patients were running about screaming, many more lay dead. (A colleague working in the laboratory to which Dr. Sasaki had been walking was dead; Dr. Sasaki's patient, whom he had just left and who a few moments before had been dreadfully afraid of syphilis, was also dead.) Dr. Sasaki found himself the only doctor in the hospital who was unhurt.

Dr. Sasaki, who believed that the enemy had hit only the building he was in, got bandages and began to bind the wounds of those inside the hospital; while outside, all over Hiroshima, maimed and dying citizens turned their unsteady steps toward the Red Cross Hospital to begin an invasion that was to make Dr. Sasaki forget his private nightmare for a long, long time.

MISS TOSHIKO SASAKI, the East Asia Tin Works clerk, who was not related to Dr. Sasaki, got up at three o'clock in the morning on the day the bomb fell. There was extra housework to do. Her eleven-month-old brother, Akio, had come down the day before with a serious stomach upset; her mother had taken him to the Tamura Pediatric Hospital and was staying there with him. Miss Sasaki, who was about twenty, had to cook breakfast for her father, a brother, a sister, and herself, and—since the hospital, because of the war, was unable to provide food—to prepare a whole day's meals for her mother and the baby, in time for her father, who worked in a factory making rubber earplugs for artillery crews, to take the food by on his way to the plant. When she had finished and had cleaned and put away the cooking things, it was nearly seven. The family lived in Koi, and she had a forty-five-minute trip to the tin works, in the section of town called Kannonmachi. She was in charge of the personnel records in the factory. She left Koi at seven, and as soon as she reached the plant, she went with some of the other girls from the personnel department to the factory auditorium. A prominent local Navy man, a former employee, had committed suicide the day before by throwing himself under a train—a death considered honorable enough to warrant a memorial service, which was to be held at the tin works at ten o'clock that morning. In the large hall, Miss Sasaki and the others made suitable preparations for the meeting. This work took about twenty minutes.

Miss Sasaki went back to her office and sat down at her desk. She was quite far from the windows, which were off to her left, and behind her were a couple of tall bookcases containing all the books of the factory library, which the personnel department had organized. She settled herself at her desk, put some things in a drawer, and shifted papers. She thought that before she began to make entries in her lists of new employees, discharges, and departures for the Army, she would chat for a moment with the girl at her right. Just as she turned her head away from the windows, the room was filled with a blinding light. She was paralyzed by fear, fixed still in her chair for a long moment (the plant was 1,600 yards from the center).

Everything fell, and Miss Sasaki lost consciousness. The ceiling dropped suddenly and the wooden floor above collapsed in splinters and the people up there came down and the roof above them gave way; but principally and first of all, the bookcases right behind her swooped forward and the contents threw her down, with her left leg horribly twisted and breaking underneath her. There, in the tin factory, in the first moment of the atomic age, a human being was crushed by books.

II · *The Fire*

IMMEDIATELY after the explosion, the Reverend Mr. Kiyoshi Tanimoto, having run wildly out of the Matsui estate and having looked in wonderment at the bloody soldiers at the mouth of the dugout they had been digging, attached himself sympathetically to an old lady who was walking along in a daze, holding her head with her left hand, supporting a small boy of three or four on her back with her right, and crying, "I'm hurt! I'm hurt! I'm hurt!" Mr. Tanimoto transferred the child to his own back and led the woman by the hand down the street, which was darkened by what seemed to be a local column of dust. He took the woman to a grammar school not far away that had previously been designated for use as a temporary hospital in case of emergency. By this solicitous behavior, Mr. Tanimoto at once got rid of his terror. At the school,

The Fire

he was much surprised to see glass all over the floor and fifty or sixty injured people already waiting to be treated. He reflected that, although the all-clear had sounded and he had heard no planes, several bombs must have been dropped. He thought of a hillock in the rayon man's garden from which he could get a view of the whole of Koi—of the whole of Hiroshima, for that matter—and he ran back up to the estate.

From the mound, Mr. Tanimoto saw an astonishing panorama. Not just a patch of Koi, as he had expected, but as much of Hiroshima as he could see through the clouded air was giving off a thick, dreadful miasma. Clumps of smoke, near and far, had begun to push up through the general dust. He wondered how such extensive damage could have been dealt out of a silent sky; even a few planes, far up, would have been audible. Houses nearby were burning, and when huge drops of water the size of marbles began to fall, he half thought that they must be coming from the hoses of firemen fighting the blazes. (They were actually drops of condensed moisture falling from the turbulent tower of dust, heat, and fission fragments that had already risen miles into the sky above Hiroshima.)

Mr. Tanimoto turned away from the sight when he heard Mr. Matsuo call out to ask whether he was all right. Mr. Matsuo had been safely cushioned within the falling house by the bedding stored in the front hall and had worked his way out. Mr. Tanimoto scarcely answered. He had thought of his wife and baby, his church, his home, his parishioners, all of them down in that awful murk. Once more he began to run in fear—toward the city.

Mrs. HATSUYO NAKAMURA, the tailor's widow, having struggled up from under the ruins of her house after the explosion, and seeing Myeko, the youngest of her three children, buried breast-deep and unable to move, crawled across the debris, hauled at timbers, and flung tiles aside, in a hurried effort to free the child. Then, from what seemed to be caverns far below, she heard two small voices crying, "*Tasukete! Tasukete!* Help! Help!"

She called the names of her ten-year-old son and eight-year-old daughter: "Toshio! Yaeko!"

The voices from below answered.

Mrs. Nakamura abandoned Myeko, who at least could breathe, and in a frenzy made the wreckage fly above the crying voices. The children had been sleeping nearly ten feet apart, but now their voices seemed to come from the same place. Toshio, the boy, apparently had some freedom to move, because she could feel him undermining the pile of wood and tiles as she worked from above. At last she saw his head, and she hastily pulled him out by it. A mosquito net was wound intricately, as if it had been carefully wrapped, around his feet. He said he had been blown right across the room and had been on top of his sister Yaeko under the wreckage. She now said, from underneath, that she could not move, because there was something on her legs. With a bit more digging, Mrs. Nakamura cleared a hole above the child and began to pull her arm. "*Itai!* It hurts!" Yaeko cried. Mrs. Nakamura shouted, "There's no time now to say whether it hurts or not," and yanked her whimpering daughter up. Then she freed Myeko. The children were filthy and bruised, but none of them had a single cut or scratch.

Mrs. Nakamura took the children out into the street. They had nothing on but underpants, and although the day was very hot, she worried rather confusedly about their being cold, so she went back into the wreckage and burrowed underneath and found a bundle of clothes she had packed for an emergency, and she dressed them in pants, blouses, shoes, padded-cotton air-raid helmets called *bokuzuki*, and even, irrationally, overcoats. The children were silent, except for the five-year-old, Myeko, who kept asking questions: "Why is it night already? Why did our house fall down? What happened?" Mrs. Nakamura, who did not know what had happened (had not the all-clear sounded?), looked around and saw through the darkness that all the houses in her neighborhood had collapsed. The house next door, which its owner had been tearing down to make way for a fire lane, was now very thoroughly, if crudely, torn down; its owner, who had been sacrificing his home for the community's safety, lay dead. Mrs. Nakamoto, wife of the head of the local air-raid-defense Neighborhood Association, came across the street with her head all bloody, and said that her baby was badly cut; did Mrs. Nakamura have any bandage? Mrs. Nakamura did not, but she crawled into the remains of her house again and pulled out some white cloth that she had been using in her work as a seamstress, ripped it into strips, and gave it to Mrs. Nakamoto. While fetching the cloth, she noticed her sewing machine; she went back in for it and dragged it out. Obviously, she could not carry it with her, so she unthinkingly plunged her symbol of livelihood into the receptacle which for weeks had been her symbol of safety—the cement tank of water in front of her house, of the type every household had been ordered to construct against a possible fire raid.

A nervous neighbor, Mrs. Hataya, called to Mrs. Nakamura to run away with her to the woods in Asano Park—an estate, by the Kyo River not far off, belonging to the wealthy Asano family, who once owned the Toyo Kisen Kaisha steamship line. The park had been designated as an evacuation area for their neighborhood. Seeing fire breaking out in a nearby ruin (except at the very center, where the bomb itself ignited some fires, most of Hiroshima's citywide conflagration was caused by inflammable wreckage falling on cookstoves and live wires), Mrs. Nakamura suggested going over to fight it. Mrs. Hataya said, "Don't be foolish. What if planes come and drop more bombs?" So Mrs. Nakamura started out for Asano Park with her children and Mrs. Hataya, and she carried her rucksack of emergency clothing, a blanket, an umbrella, and a suitcase of things she had cached in her air-raid shelter. Under many ruins, as they hurried along, they heard muffled screams for help. The only building they saw standing on their way to Asano Park was the Jesuit mission house, alongside the Catholic kindergarten to which Mrs. Nakamura had sent Myeko for a time. As they passed it, she saw Father Kleinsorge, in bloody underwear, running out of the house with a small suitcase in his hand.

RIGHT AFTER the explosion, while Father Wilhelm Kleinsorge, S.J., was wandering around in his underwear in the vegetable garden, Father Superior LaSalle came around the corner of the building in the darkness. His body, especially his back, was bloody; the flash had made him twist away from his window, and tiny pieces of glass had flown at him. Father Kleinsorge, still bewildered, managed to ask, "Where are the rest?" Just then, the two other priests living in the mission house appeared—Father Cieslik, unhurt, supporting Father Schiffer, who was covered with blood that spurted from a cut above his left ear and who was very pale. Father Cieslik was rather pleased with himself, for after the flash he had dived into a doorway, which he had previously reckoned to be the safest place inside the building, and when the blast came, he was not injured. Father LaSalle told Father Cieslik to take Father Schiffer to a doctor before he bled to death, and suggested either Dr. Kanda, who lived on the next corner, or Dr. Fujii, about six blocks away. The two men went out of the compound and up the street.

The daughter of Mr. Hoshijima, the mission catechist, ran up to Father Kleinsorge and said that her mother and sister were buried under the ruins of their house, which was at the back of the Jesuit compound, and at the same time the priests noticed that the house of the Catholic-kindergarten teacher at the front of the compound had collapsed on her. While Father LaSalle and Mrs. Murata, the mission housekeeper, dug the teacher out, Father Kleinsorge went to the catechist's fallen house and began lifting things off the top of the pile. There was not a sound underneath; he was sure the Hoshijima women had been killed. At last, under what had been a corner of the kitchen, he saw Mrs. Hoshijima's head. Believing her dead, he began to haul her out by the hair, but suddenly she screamed, *"Itai! Itai!* It hurts! It hurts!" He dug some more and lifted her out. He managed, too, to find her daughter in the rubble and free her. Neither was badly hurt.

A public bath next door to the mission house had caught fire, but since there the wind was southerly, the priests thought their house would be spared. Nevertheless, as a precaution, Father Kleinsorge went inside to fetch some things he wanted to save. He found his room in a state of weird and illogical confusion. A first-aid kit was hanging undisturbed on a hook on the wall, but his clothes, which had been on other hooks nearby, were nowhere to be seen. His desk was in splinters all over the room, but a mere papier-mâché suitcase, which he had hidden under the desk, stood handle-side up, without a scratch on it, in the doorway of the room, where he could not miss it. Father Kleinsorge later

The Fire

came to regard this as a bit of Providential interference, inasmuch as the suitcase contained his breviary, the account books for the whole diocese, and a considerable amount of paper money belonging to the mission, for which he was responsible. He ran out of the house and deposited the suitcase in the mission air-raid shelter.

At about this time, Father Cieslik and Father Schiffer, who was still spurting blood, came back and said that Dr. Kanda's house was ruined and that fire blocked them from getting out of what they supposed to be the local circle of destruction to Dr. Fujii's private hospital, on the bank of the Kyo River.

Dr. Masakazu Fujii's hospital was no longer on the bank of the Kyo River; it was in the river. After the overturn, Dr. Fujii was so stupefied and so tightly squeezed by the beams gripping his chest that he was unable to move at first, and he hung there about twenty minutes in the darkened morning. Then a thought which came to him—that soon the tide would be running in through the estuaries and his head would be submerged—inspired him to fearful activity; he wriggled and turned and exerted what strength he could (though his left arm, because of the pain in his shoulder, was useless), and before long he had freed himself from the vise. After a few moments' rest, he climbed onto the pile of timbers and, finding a long one that slanted up to the riverbank, he painfully shinnied up it.

Dr. Fujii, who was in his underwear, was now soaking and dirty. His undershirt was torn, and blood ran down it from bad cuts on his chin and back. In this disarray, he walked out onto Kyo Bridge, beside which his hospital had stood. The bridge had not collapsed. He could see only fuzzily without his glasses, but he could see enough to be amazed at the number of houses that were down all around. On the bridge, he encountered a friend, a doctor named Machii, and asked in bewilderment, "What do you think it was?"

Dr. Machii said, "It must have been a *Molotoffano hanakago*"—a Molotov flower basket, the delicate Japanese name for the "bread basket," or self-scattering cluster of bombs.

At first, Dr. Fujii could see only two fires, one across the river from his hospital site and one quite far to the south. But at the same time, he and his friend observed something that puzzled them, and which, as doctors, they discussed: although there were as yet very few fires, wounded people were hurrying across the bridge in an endless parade of misery, and many of them exhibited terrible burns on their faces and arms. "Why do you suppose it is?" Dr. Fujii asked. Even a theory was comforting that day, and Dr. Machii stuck to his. "Perhaps because it was a Molotov flower basket," he said.

There had been no breeze earlier in the morning when Dr. Fujii had walked to the railway station to see his friend off, but now brisk winds were blowing every which way; here on the bridge the wind was easterly. New fires were leaping up, and they spread quickly, and in a very short time terrible blasts of hot air and showers of cinders made it impossible to stand on the bridge any more. Dr. Machii ran to the far side of the river and along a still unkindled street. Dr. Fujii went down into the water under the bridge, where a score of people had already taken refuge, among them his servants, who had extricated themselves from the wreckage. From there, Dr. Fujii saw a nurse hanging in the timbers of his hospital by her legs, and then another painfully pinned across the breast. He enlisted the help of some of the others under the bridge and freed both of them. He thought he heard the voice of his niece for a moment, but he could not find her; he never saw her again. Four of his nurses and the two patients in the hospital died, too. Dr. Fujii went back into the water of the river and waited for the fire to subside.

THE LOT of Drs. Fujii, Kanda, and Machii right after the explosion—and, as these three were typical, that of the majority of the physicians and surgeons of Hiroshima—with their offices and hospitals destroyed, their equipment scattered, their own bodies incapacitated in varying degrees, explained why so many citizens who were hurt went untended and why so many who might have lived died. Of a hundred and fifty doctors in the city, sixty-five were already dead and most of the rest were wounded. Of 1,780 nurses, 1,654 were dead or too badly hurt to work. In the biggest hospital, that of the Red Cross, only six doctors out of thirty were able to function, and only ten nurses out of more than two hundred. The sole uninjured doctor on the Red Cross Hospital staff was Dr. Sasaki. After the explosion, he hurried to a storeroom to fetch bandages. This room, like everything he had seen as he ran through the hospital, was chaotic—bottles of medicines thrown off shelves and broken, salves spattered on the walls, instruments strewn everywhere. He grabbed up some bandages and an unbroken bottle of Mercurochrome, hurried back to the chief surgeon, and bandaged his cuts. Then he went out into the corridor and began patching up the wounded patients and the doctors and nurses there. He blundered so without his glasses that he took a pair off the face of a wounded nurse, and although they only approximately compensated for the errors of his vision, they were better than nothing. (He was to depend on them for more than a month.)

Dr. Sasaki worked without method, taking those who were nearest him first, and he noticed soon that the corridor seemed to be getting more and more crowded. Mixed in with the abrasions and lacerations which most people in the hospital had suffered, he began to find dreadful burns. He realized then that casualties were pouring in from outdoors. There were so many that he began to pass up the lightly wounded; he decided that all he could hope to do was to stop people from bleeding to death. Before long, patients lay and crouched on the floors of the wards and the laboratories and all the other rooms, and in the corridors, and on the stairs, and in the front hall, and under the porte-cochère, and on the stone front steps, and in the drive-

The Fire

way and courtyard, and for blocks each way in the streets outside. Wounded people supported maimed people; disfigured families leaned together. Many people were vomiting. A tremendous number of schoolgirls—some of those who had been taken from their classrooms to work outdoors, clearing fire lanes—crept into the hospital. In a city of two hundred and forty-five thousand, nearly a hundred thousand people had been killed or doomed at one blow; a hundred thousand more were hurt. At least ten thousand of the wounded made their way to the best hospital in town, which was altogether unequal to such a trampling, since it had only six hundred beds, and they had all been occupied. The people in the suffocating crowd inside the hospital wept and cried, for Dr. Sasaki to hear, "*Sensei!* Doctor!," and the less seriously wounded came and pulled at his sleeve and begged him to go to the aid of the worse wounded. Tugged here and there in his stockinged feet, bewildered by the numbers, staggered by so much raw flesh, Dr. Sasaki lost all sense of profession and stopped working as a skillful surgeon and a sympathetic man; he became an automaton, mechanically wiping, daubing, winding, wiping, daubing, winding.

SOME OF the wounded in Hiroshima were unable to enjoy the questionable luxury of hospitalization. In what had been the personnel office of the East Asia Tin Works, Miss Sasaki lay doubled over, unconscious, under the tremendous pile of books and plaster and wood and corrugated iron. She was wholly unconscious (she later estimated) for about three hours. Her first sensation was of dreadful pain in her left leg. It was so black under the books and debris that the borderline between awareness and unconsciousness was fine; she apparently crossed it several times, for the pain seemed to come and go. At the moments when it was sharpest, she felt that her leg had been cut off somewhere below the knee. Later, she heard someone walking on top of the wreckage above her, and anguished voices spoke up, evidently from within the mess around her: "Please help! Get us out!"

FATHER KLEINSORGE stemmed Father Schiffer's spurting cut as well as he could with some bandage that Dr. Fujii had given the priests a few days before. When he finished, he ran into the mission house again and found the jacket of his military uniform and an old pair of gray trousers. He put them on and went outside. A woman from next door ran up to him and shouted that her husband was buried under her house and the house was on fire; Father Kleinsorge must come and save him.

Father Kleinsorge, already growing apathetic and dazed in the presence of the cumulative distress, said, "We haven't much time." Houses all around were burning, and the wind was now blowing hard. "Do you know exactly which part of the house he is under?" he asked.

"Yes, yes," she said. "Come quickly."

The Fire

They went around to the house, the remains of which blazed violently, but when they got there, it turned out that the woman had no idea where her husband was. Father Kleinsorge shouted several times, "Is anyone there?" There was no answer. Father Kleinsorge said to the woman, "We must get away or we will all die." He went back to the Catholic compound and told the Father Superior that the fire was coming closer on the wind, which had swung around and was now from the north; it was time for everybody to go.

Just then, the kindergarten teacher pointed out to the priests Mr. Fukai, the secretary of the diocese, who was standing in his window on the second floor of the mission house, facing in the direction of the explosion, weeping. Father Cieslik, because he thought the stairs unusable, ran around to the back of the mission house to look for a ladder. There he heard people crying for help under a nearby fallen roof. He called to passers-by running away in the street to help him lift it, but nobody paid any attention, and he had to leave the buried ones to die. Father Kleinsorge ran inside the mission house and scrambled up the stairs, which were awry and piled with plaster and lathing, and called to Mr. Fukai from the doorway of his room.

Mr. Fukai, a very short man of about fifty, turned around slowly, with a queer look, and said, "Leave me here."

Father Kleinsorge went into the room and took Mr. Fukai by the collar of his coat and said, "Come with me or you'll die."

Mr. Fukai said, "Leave me here to die."

Father Kleinsorge began to shove and haul Mr. Fukai out of the room. Then the theological student came up and grabbed Mr. Fukai's feet, and Father Kleinsorge took his shoulders, and together they carried him downstairs and outdoors. "I can't walk!" Mr. Fukai cried. "Leave me here!" Father Kleinsorge got his paper suitcase with the money in it and took Mr. Fukai up pickaback, and the party started for the East Parade Ground, their district's "safe area." As they went out of the gate, Mr. Fukai, quite childlike now, beat on Father Kleinsorge's shoulders and said, "I won't leave. I won't leave." Irrelevantly, Father Kleinsorge turned to Father LaSalle and said, "We have lost all our possessions but not our sense of humor."

The street was cluttered with parts of houses that had slid into it, and with fallen telephone poles and wires. From every second or third house came the voices of people buried and abandoned, who invariably screamed, with formal politeness, *Tasukete kure!* Help, if you please!" The priests recognized several ruins from which these cries came as the homes of friends, but because of the fire it was too late to help. All the way, Mr. Fukai whimpered, "Let me stay." The party turned right when they came to a block of fallen houses that was one flame. At Sakai Bridge, which would take them across to the East Parade Ground, they saw that the whole community on the opposite side of the river was a sheet of fire; they dared not cross and decided to take refuge in Asano Park, off to their

The Fire

left. Father Kleinsorge, who had been weakened for a couple of days by his bad case of diarrhea, began to stagger under his protesting burden, and as he tried to climb up over the wreckage of several houses that blocked their way to the park, he stumbled, dropped Mr. Fukai, and plunged down, head over heels, to the edge of the river. When he picked himself up, he saw Mr. Fukai running away. Father Kleinsorge shouted to a dozen soldiers, who were standing by the bridge, to stop him. As Father Kleinsorge started back to get Mr. Fukai, Father LaSalle called out, "Hurry! Don't waste time!" So Father Kleinsorge just requested the soldiers to take care of Mr. Fukai. They said they would, but the little, broken man got away from them, and the last the priests could see of him, he was running back toward the fire.

Mr. Tanimoto, fearful for his family and church, at first ran toward them by the shortest route, along Koi Highway. He was the only person making his way into the city; he met hundreds and hundreds who were fleeing, and every one of them seemed to be hurt in some way. The eyebrows of some were burned off and skin hung from their faces and hands. Others, because of pain, held their arms up as if carrying something in both hands. Some were vomiting as they walked. Many were naked or in shreds of clothing. On some undressed bodies, the burns had made patterns—of undershirt straps and suspenders and, on the skin of some women (since white repelled the heat from the bomb and dark clothes absorbed it and conducted it to the skin), the shapes of flowers they had had on their kimonos. Many, although injured themselves, supported relatives who were worse off. Almost all had their heads bowed, looked straight ahead, were silent, and showed no expression whatever.

After crossing Koi Bridge and Kannon Bridge, having run the whole way, Mr. Tanimoto saw, as he approached the center, that all the houses had been crushed and many were afire. Here the trees were bare and their trunks were charred. He tried at several points to penetrate the ruins, but the flames always stopped him. Under many houses, people screamed for help, but no one helped; in general, survivors that day assisted only their relatives or immediate neighbors, for they could not comprehend or tolerate a wider circle of misery. The wounded limped past the screams, and Mr. Tanimoto ran past them. As a Christian he was filled with compassion for those who were trapped, and as a Japanese he was overwhelmed by the shame of being unhurt, and he prayed as he ran, "God help them and take them out of the fire."

He thought he would skirt the fire, to the left. He ran back to Kannon Bridge and followed for a distance one of the rivers. He tried several cross streets, but all were blocked, so he turned far left and ran out to Yokogawa, a station on a railroad line that detoured the city in a wide semicircle, and he followed the rails until he came to a burning train. So impressed was he by this time by the extent of the damage that he ran

The Fire

north two miles to Gion, a suburb in the foothills. All the way, he overtook dreadfully burned and lacerated people, and in his guilt he turned to right and left as he hurried and said to some of them, "Excuse me for having no burden like yours." Near Gion, he began to meet country people going toward the city to help, and when they saw him, several exclaimed, "Look! There is one who is not wounded." At Gion, he bore toward the right bank of the main river, the Ota, and ran down it until he reached fire again. There was no fire on the other side of the river, so he threw off his shirt and shoes and plunged into it. In midstream, where the current was fairly strong, exhaustion and fear finally caught up with him—he had run nearly seven miles—and he became limp and drifted in the water. He prayed, "Please, God, help me to cross. It would be nonsense for me to be drowned when I am the only uninjured one." He managed a few more strokes and fetched up on a spit downstream.

Mr. Tanimoto climbed up the bank and ran along it until, near a large Shinto shrine, he came to more fire, and as he turned left to get around it, he met, by incredible luck, his wife. She was carrying their infant daughter. Mr. Tanimoto was now so emotionally worn out that nothing could surprise him. He did not embrace his wife; he simply said, "Oh, you are safe." She told him that she had got home from her night in Ushida just in time for the explosion; she had been buried under the parsonage with the baby in her arms. She told how the wreckage had pressed down on her, how the baby had cried. She saw a chink of light, and by reaching up with a hand, she worked the hole bigger, bit by bit. After about half an hour, she heard the crackling noise of wood burning. At last the opening was big enough for her to push the baby out, and afterward she crawled out herself. She said she was now going out to Ushida again. Mr. Tanimoto said he wanted to see his church and take care of the people of his Neighborhood Association. They parted as casually—as bewildered—as they had met.

Mr. Tanimoto's way around the fire took him across the East Parade Ground, which, being an evacuation area, was now the scene of a gruesome review: rank on rank of the burned and bleeding. Those who were burned moaned, *"Mizu, mizu!* Water, water!" Mr. Tanimoto found a basin in a nearby street and located a water tap that still worked in the crushed shell of a house, and he began carrying water to the suffering strangers. When he had given drink to about thirty of them, he realized he was taking too much time. "Excuse me," he said loudly to those nearby who were reaching out their hands to him and crying their thirst. "I have many people to take care of." Then he ran away. He went to the river again, the basin in his hand, and jumped down onto a sandspit. There he saw hundreds of people so badly wounded that they could not get up to go farther from the burning city. When they saw a man erect and unhurt, the chant began again: *"Mizu, mizu, mizu."* Mr. Tanimoto could not resist them; he carried them water from the river—a mis-

The Fire

take, since it was tidal and brackish. Two or three small boats were ferrying hurt people across the river from Asano Park, and when one touched the spit, Mr. Tanimoto again made his loud, apologetic speech and jumped into the boat. It took him across to the park. There, in the underbrush, he found some of his charges of the Neighborhood Association, who had come there by his previous instructions, and saw many acquaintances, among them Father Kleinsorge and the other Catholics. But he missed Fukai, who had been a close friend. "Where is Fukai-*san*?" he asked.

"He didn't want to come with us," Father Kleinsorge said. "He ran back."

WHEN MISS SASAKI heard the voices of the people caught along with her in the dilapidation at the tin factory, she began speaking to them. Her nearest neighbor, she discovered, was a high-school girl who had been drafted for factory work, and who said her back was broken. Miss Sasaki replied, "I am lying here and I can't move. My left leg is cut off."

Some time later, she again heard somebody walk overhead and then move off to one side, and whoever it was began burrowing. The digger released several people, and when he had uncovered the high-school girl, she found that her back was not broken, after all, and she crawled out. Miss Sasaki spoke to the rescuer, and he worked toward her. He pulled away a great number of books, until he had made a tunnel to her. She could see his perspiring face as he said, "Come out, Miss." She tried. "I can't move," she said. The man excavated some more and told her to try with all her strength to get out. But books were heavy on her hips, and the man finally saw that a bookcase was leaning on the books and that a heavy beam pressed down on the bookcase. "Wait," he said. "I'll get a crowbar."

The man was gone a long time, and when he came back, he was ill-tempered, as if her plight were all her fault. "We have no men to help you!" he shouted in through the tunnel. "You'll have to get out by yourself."

"That's impossible," she said. "My left leg . . ." The man went away.

Much later, several men came and dragged Miss Sasaki out. Her left leg was not severed, but it was badly broken and cut and it hung askew below the knee. They took her out into a courtyard. It was raining. She sat on the ground in the rain. When the downpour increased, someone directed all the wounded people to take cover in the factory's air-raid shelters. "Come along," a torn-up woman said to her. "You can hop." But Miss Sasaki could not move, and she just waited in the rain. Then a man propped up a large sheet of corrugated iron as a kind of lean-to, and took her in his arms and carried her to it. She was grateful until he brought two horribly wounded people—a woman with a whole breast sheared off and a man whose face was all raw from a burn—to share the simple shed with her. No one came back. The rain cleared and the cloudy afternoon was hot; before nightfall the three grotesques under the slanting piece of twisted iron began to smell quite bad.

THE FORMER head of the Nobori-cho Neighborhood Association to which the Catholic priests belonged was an energetic man named Yoshida. He had boasted, when he was in charge of the district air-raid defenses, that fire might eat away all of Hiroshima but it would never come to Nobori-cho. The bomb blew down his house, and a joist pinned him by the legs, in full view of the Jesuit mission house across the way and of the people hurrying along the street. In their confusion as they hurried past, Mrs. Nakamura, with her children, and Father Kleinsorge, with Mr. Fukai on his back, hardly saw him; he was just part of the general blur of misery through which they moved. His cries for help brought no response from them; there were so many people shouting for help that they could not hear him separately. They and all the others went along. Nobori-cho became absolutely deserted, and the fire swept through it. Mr. Yoshida saw the wooden mission house—the only erect building in the area—go up in a lick of flame, and the heat was terrific on his face. Then flames came along his side of the street and entered his house. In a paroxysm of terrified strength, he freed himself and ran down the alleys of Nobori-cho, hemmed in by the fire he had said would never come. He began at once to behave like an old man; two months later his hair was white.

As Dr. Fujii stood in the river up to his neck to avoid the heat of the fire, the wind blew stronger and stronger, and soon, even though the expanse of water was small, the waves grew so high that the people under the bridge could no longer keep their footing. Dr. Fujii went close to the shore, crouched down, and embraced a large stone with his usable arm. Later it became possible to wade along the very edge of the river, and Dr. Fujii and his two surviving nurses moved about two hundred yards upstream, to a sandspit near Asano Park. Many wounded were lying on the sand. Dr. Machii was there with his family; his daughter, who had been outdoors when the bomb burst, was badly burned on her hands and legs but fortunately not on her face. Although Dr. Fujii's shoulder was by now terribly painful, he examined the girl's burns curiously. Then he lay down. In spite of the misery all around, he was ashamed of his appearance, and he remarked to Dr. Machii that he looked like a beggar, dressed as he was in nothing but torn and bloody underwear. Later in the afternoon, when the fire began to subside, he decided to go to his parental house, in the suburb of Nagatsuka. He asked Dr. Machii to join him, but the Doctor answered that he and his family were going to spend the night on the spit, because of his daughter's injuries. Dr. Fujii, together with his nurses, walked first to Ushida, where, in the partially damaged house of some relatives, he found first-aid materials he had stored there. The two nurses bandaged him and he them. They went on. Now not many people walked in the streets, but a great number sat and lay on the pavement, vomited, waited for death, and died. The number of corpses on the way to Nagatsuka was more and more puzzling. The Doctor wondered: Could a Molotov flower basket have done all this?

Dr. Fujii reached his family's house in the evening. It was five miles from the center of town, but its roof had fallen in and the windows were all broken.

ALL DAY, people poured into Asano Park. This private estate was far enough away from the explosion so that its bamboos, pines, laurel, and maples were still alive, and the green place invited refugees—partly because they believed that if the Americans came back, they would bomb only buildings; partly because the foliage seemed a center of coolness and life, and the estate's exquisitely precise rock gardens, with their quiet pools and arching bridges, were very Japanese, normal, secure; and also partly (according to some who were there) because of an irresistible, atavistic urge to hide under leaves. Mrs. Nakamura and her children were among the first to arrive, and they settled in the bamboo grove near the river. They all felt terribly thirsty, and they drank from the river. At once they were nauseated and began vomiting, and they retched the whole day. Others were also nauseated; they all thought (probably because of the strong odor of ionization, an "electric smell" given off by the bomb's fission) that they were sick from a gas the Americans had dropped. When Father Kleinsorge and the other priests came into the park, nodding to their friends as they passed, the Nakamuras were all sick and prostrate. A woman named Iwasaki, who lived in the neighborhood of the mission and who was sitting near the Nakamuras, got up and asked the priests if she should stay where she was or go with them. Father Kleinsorge said, "I hardly know where the safest place is." She stayed there, and later in the day, though she had no visible wounds or burns, she died. The priests went farther along the river and settled down in some underbrush. Father LaSalle lay down and went right to sleep. The theological student, who was wearing slippers, had carried with him a bundle of clothes, in which he had packed two pairs of leather shoes. When he sat down with the others, he found that the bundle had broken open and a couple of shoes had fallen out and now he had only two lefts. He retraced his steps and found one right. When he rejoined the priests, he said, "It's funny, but things don't matter any more. Yesterday, my shoes were my most important possessions. Today, I don't care. One pair is enough."

Father Cieslik said, "I know. I started to bring my books along, and then I thought, 'This is no time for books.' "

When Mr. Tanimoto, with his basin still in his hand, reached the park, it was very crowded, and to distinguish the living from the dead was not easy, for most of the people lay still, with their eyes open. To

The Fire

Father Kleinsorge, an Occidental, the silence in the grove by the river, where hundreds of gruesomely wounded suffered together, was one of the most dreadful and awesome phenomena of his whole experience. The hurt ones were quiet; no one wept, much less screamed in pain; no one complained; none of the many who died did so noisily; not even the children cried; very few people even spoke. And when Father Kleinsorge gave water to some whose faces had been almost blotted out by flash burns, they took their share and then raised themselves a little and bowed to him, in thanks.

Mr. Tanimoto greeted the priests and then looked around for other friends. He saw Mrs. Matsumoto, wife of the director of the Methodist School, and asked her if she was thirsty. She was, so he went to one of the pools in the Asano rock gardens and got water for her in his basin. Then he decided to try to get back to his church. He went into Nobori-cho by the way the priests had taken as they escaped, but he did not get far; the fire along the streets was so fierce that he had to turn back. He walked to the riverbank and began to look for a boat in which he might carry some of the most severely injured across the river from Asano Park and away from the spreading fire. Soon he found a good-sized pleasure punt drawn up on the bank, but in and around it was an awful tableau—five dead men, nearly naked, badly burned, who must have expired more or less all at once, for they were in attitudes which suggested that they had been working together to push the boat down into the river. Mr. Tanimoto lifted them away from the boat, and as he did so, he experienced such horror at disturbing the dead—preventing them, he momentarily felt, from launching their craft and going on their ghostly way—that he said out loud, "Please forgive me for taking this boat. I must use it for others, who are alive." The punt was heavy, but he managed to slide it into the water. There were no oars, and all he could find for propulsion was a thick bamboo pole. He worked the boat upstream to the most crowded part of the park and began to ferry the wounded. He could pack ten or twelve into the boat for each crossing, but as the river was too deep in the center to pole his way across, he had to paddle with the bamboo, and consequently each trip took a very long time. He worked several hours that way.

Early in the afternoon, the fire swept into the woods of Asano Park. The first Mr. Tanimoto knew of it was when, returning in his boat, he saw that a great number of people had moved toward the riverside. On touching the bank, he went up to investigate, and when he saw the fire, he shouted, "All the young men who are not badly hurt come with me!" Father Kleinsorge moved Father Schiffer and Father LaSalle close to the edge of the river and asked people there to get them across if the fire came too near, and then joined Tanimoto's volunteers. Mr. Tanimoto sent some to look for buckets and basins and told others to beat the burning underbrush with their clothes; when utensils were at hand, he formed a bucket chain from one of the pools

The Fire

in the rock gardens. The team fought the fire for more than two hours, and gradually defeated the flames. As Mr. Tanimoto's men worked, the frightened people in the park pressed closer and closer to the river, and finally the mob began to force some of the unfortunates who were on the very bank into the water. Among those driven into the river and drowned were Mrs. Matsumoto, of the Methodist School, and her daughter.

When Father Kleinsorge got back after fighting the fire, he found Father Schiffer still bleeding and terribly pale. Some Japanese stood around and stared at him, and Father Schiffer whispered, with a weak smile, "It is as if I were already dead." "Not yet," Father Kleinsorge said. He had brought Dr. Fujii's first-aid kit with him, and he had noticed Dr. Kanda in the crowd, so he sought him out and asked him if he would dress Father Schiffer's bad cuts. Dr. Kanda had seen his wife and daughter dead in the ruins of his hospital; he sat now with his head in his hands. "I can't do anything," he said. Father Kleinsorge bound more bandage around Father Schiffer's head, moved him to a steep place, and settled him so that his head was high, and soon the bleeding diminished.

The roar of approaching planes was heard about this time. Someone in the crowd near the Nakamura family shouted, "It's some Grummans coming to strafe us!" A baker named Nakashima stood up and commanded, "Everyone who is wearing anything white, take it off." Mrs. Nakamura took the blouses off her children, and opened her umbrella and made them get under it. A great number of people, even badly burned ones, crawled into bushes and stayed there until the hum, evidently of a reconnaissance or weather run, died away.

It began to rain. Mrs. Nakamura kept her children under the umbrella. The drops grew abnormally large, and someone shouted, "The Americans are dropping gasoline. They're going to set fire to us!" (This alarm stemmed from one of the theories being passed through the park as to why so much of Hiroshima had burned: it was that a single plane had sprayed gasoline on the city and then somehow set fire to it in one flashing moment.) But the drops were palpably water, and as they fell, the wind grew stronger and stronger, and suddenly—probably because of the tremendous convection set up by the blazing city—a whirlwind ripped through the park. Huge trees crashed down; small ones were uprooted and flew into the air. Higher, a wild array of flat things revolved in the twisting funnel—pieces of iron roofing, papers, doors, strips of matting. Father Kleinsorge put a piece of cloth over Father Schiffer's eyes, so that the feeble man would not think he was going crazy. The gale blew Mrs. Murata, the mission housekeeper, who was sitting close by the river, down the embankment at a shallow, rocky place, and she came out with her bare feet bloody. The vortex moved out onto the river, where it sucked up a waterspout and eventually spent itself.

After the storm, Mr. Tanimoto began ferrying

The Fire

people again, and Father Kleinsorge asked the theological student to go across and make his way out to the Jesuit Novitiate at Nagatsuka, about three miles from the center of town, and to request the priests there to come with help for Fathers Schiffer and La-Salle. The student got into Mr. Tanimoto's boat and went off with him. Father Kleinsorge asked Mrs. Nakamura if she would like to go out to Nagatsuka with the priests when they came. She said she had some luggage and her children were sick—they were still vomiting from time to time, and so, for that matter, was she—and therefore she feared she could not. He said he thought the fathers from the Novitiate could come back the next day with a pushcart to get her.

Late in the afternoon, when he went ashore for a while, Mr. Tanimoto, upon whose energy and initiative many had come to depend, heard people begging for food. He consulted Father Kleinsorge, and they decided to go back into town to get some rice from Mr. Tanimoto's Neighborhood Association shelter and from the mission shelter. Father Cieslik and two or three others went with them. At first, when they got among the rows of prostrate houses, they did not know where they were; the change was too sudden, from a busy city of two hundred and forty-five thousand that morning to a mere pattern of residue in the afternoon. The asphalt of the streets was still so soft and hot from the fires that walking was uncomfortable. They encountered only one person, a woman, who said to them as they passed, "My husband is in those ashes."

At the mission, where Mr. Tanimoto left the party, Father Kleinsorge was dismayed to see the building razed. In the garden, on the way to the shelter, he noticed a pumpkin roasted on the vine. He and Father Cieslik tasted it and it was good. They were surprised at their hunger, and they ate quite a bit. They got out several bags of rice and gathered up several other cooked pumpkins and dug up some potatoes that were nicely baked under the ground, and started back. Mr. Tanimoto rejoined them on the way. One of the people with him had some cooking utensils. In the park, Mr. Tanimoto organized the lightly wounded women of his neighborhood to cook. Father Kleinsorge offered the Nakamura family some pumpkin, and they tried it, but they could not keep it on their stomachs. Altogether, the rice was enough to feed nearly a hundred people.

Just before dark, Mr. Tanimoto came across a twenty-year-old girl, Mrs. Kamai, the Tanimoto's next-door neighbor. She was crouching on the ground with the body of her infant daughter in her arms. The baby had evidently been dead all day. Mrs. Kamai jumped up when she saw Mr. Tanimoto and said, "Would you please try to locate my husband?"

Mr. Tanimoto knew that her husband had been inducted into the Army just the day before; he and Mrs. Tanimoto had entertained Mrs. Kamai in the afternoon, to make her forget. Kamai had reported to the Chugoku Regional Army Headquarters—near the ancient castle in the middle of town—where some four thousand troops were stationed. Judging by the many maimed soldiers Mr. Tanimoto had seen during the day, he surmised that the barracks had been badly damaged by whatever it was that had hit Hiroshima. He knew he hadn't a chance of finding Mrs. Kamai's husband, even if he searched, but he wanted to humor her. "I'll try," he said.

"You've got to find him," she said. "He loved our baby so much. I want him to see her once more."

III · *Details Are Being Investigated*

Early in the evening of the day the bomb exploded, a Japanese naval launch moved slowly up and down the seven rivers of Hiroshima. It stopped here and there to make an announcement—alongside the crowded sandspits, on which hundreds of wounded lay; at the bridges, on which others were crowded; and eventually, as twilight fell, opposite Asano Park. A young officer stood up in the launch and shouted through a megaphone, "Be patient! A naval hospital ship is coming to take care of you!" The sight of the shipshape launch against the background of the havoc across the river; the unruffled young man in his neat uniform; above all, the promise of medical help—the first word of possible succor anyone had heard in nearly twelve awful hours—cheered the people in the park tremendously. Mrs. Nakamura settled her family for the night with the assurance that a doctor would come and stop their retching. Mr. Tanimoto resumed ferrying the wounded across the river. Father Kleinsorge lay down and said the Lord's Prayer and a Hail Mary to himself, and fell right asleep; but no sooner had he dropped off than Mrs. Murata, the conscientious mission housekeeper, shook him and said, "Father Kleinsorge! Did you remember to repeat your evening prayers?" He answered rather grumpily, "Of course," and he tried to go back to sleep but could not. This, apparently, was just what Mrs. Murata wanted. She began to chat with the exhausted priest. One of the questions she raised was when he thought the priests from the Novitiate, for whom he had sent a messenger in midafternoon, would arrive to evacuate Father Superior LaSalle and Father Schiffer.

THE MESSENGER Father Kleinsorge had sent—the theological student who had been living at the mission house—had arrived at the Novitiate, in the hills about three miles out, at half past four. The sixteen priests there had been doing rescue work in the outskirts; they had worried about their colleagues in the city but had not known how or where to look for them. Now they hastily made two litters out of poles and boards, and the student led half a dozen of them back into the devastated area. They worked their way along the Ota above the city; twice the heat of the fire forced them into the river. At Misasa Bridge, they encountered a long line of soldiers making a bizarre forced march away from the Chugoku Regional Army Head-

quarters in the center of the town. All were gro-
tesquely burned, and they supported themselves with
staves or leaned on one another. Sick, burned horses,
hanging their heads, stood on the bridge. When the
rescue party reached the park, it was after dark, and
progress was made extremely difficult by the tangle of
fallen trees of all sizes that had been knocked down by
the whirlwind that afternoon. At last—not long after
Mrs. Murata asked her question—they reached their
friends, and gave them wine and strong tea.

The priests discussed how to get Father Schiffer and
Father LaSalle out to the Novitiate. They were afraid
that blundering through the park with them would
jar them too much on the wooden litters, and that the
wounded men would lose too much blood. Father
Kleinsorge thought of Mr. Tanimoto and his boat, and
called out to him on the river. When Mr. Tanimoto
reached the bank, he said he would be glad to take the
injured priests and their bearers upstream to where
they could find a clear roadway. The rescuers put
Father Schiffer onto one of the stretchers and lowered
it into the boat, and two of them went aboard with it.
Mr. Tanimoto, who still had no oars, poled the punt
upstream.

About half an hour later, Mr. Tanimoto came back
and excitedly asked the remaining priests to help him
rescue two children he had seen standing up to their
shoulders in the river. A group went out and picked
them up—two young girls who had lost their family

and were both badly burned. The priests stretched them on the ground next to Father Kleinsorge and then embarked Father LaSalle. Father Cieslik thought he could make it out to the Novitiate on foot, so he went aboard with the others. Father Kleinsorge was too feeble; he decided to wait in the park until the next day. He asked the men to come back with a hand-cart, so that they could take Mrs. Nakamura and her sick children to the Novitiate.

Mr. Tanimoto shoved off again. As the boatload of priests moved slowly upstream, they heard weak cries for help. A woman's voice stood out especially: "There are people here about to be drowned! Help us! The water is rising!" The sounds came from one of the sandspits, and those in the punt could see, in the re-flected light of the still-burning fires, a number of wounded people lying at the edge of the river, already partly covered by the flooding tide. Mr. Tanimoto wanted to help them, but the priests were afraid that Father Schiffer would die if they didn't hurry, and they urged their ferryman along. He dropped them where he had put Father Schiffer down and then started back alone toward the sandspit.

THE NIGHT was hot, and it seemed even hotter be-cause of the fires against the sky, but the younger of the two girls Mr. Tanimoto and the priests had res-cued complained to Father Kleinsorge that she was cold. He covered her with his jacket. She and her older sister had been in the salt water of the river for a couple of hours before being rescued. The younger one had huge, raw flash burns on her body; the salt water must have been excruciatingly painful to her. She began to shiver heavily, and again said it was cold. Father Kleinsorge borrowed a blanket from someone nearby and wrapped her up, but she shook more and more, and said again, "I am so cold," and then she suddenly stopped shivering and was dead.

MR. TANIMOTO found about twenty men and women on the sandspit. He drove the boat onto the bank and urged them to get aboard. They did not move and he realized that they were too weak to lift themselves. He reached down and took a woman by the hands, but her skin slipped off in huge, glovelike pieces. He was so sickened by this that he had to sit down for a moment. Then he got out into the water and, though a small man, lifted several of the men and women, who were naked, into his boat. Their backs and breasts were clammy, and he remembered uneasily what the great burns he had seen during the day had been like: yellow at first, then red and swollen, with the skin sloughed off, and finally, in the evening, suppurated and smelly. With the tide risen, his bamboo pole was now too short and he had to paddle most of the way across with it. On the other side, at a higher spit, he lifted the slimy living bodies out and carried them up the slope away from the tide. He had to keep con-

sciously repeating to himself, "These are human beings." It took him three trips to get them all across the
river. When he had finished, he decided he had to have
a rest, and he went back to the park.

As Mr. Tanimoto stepped up the dark bank, he
tripped over someone, and someone else said angrily,
"Look out! That's my hand." Mr. Tanimoto, ashamed
of hurting wounded people, embarrassed at being able
to walk upright, suddenly thought of the naval hospital ship, which had not come (it never did), and he
had for a moment a feeling of blind, murderous rage at
the crew of the ship, and then at all doctors. Why
didn't they come to help these people?

Dr. Fujii lay in dreadful pain throughout the night
on the floor of his family's roofless house on the edge
of the city. By the light of a lantern, he had examined
himself and found: left clavicle fractured; multiple
abrasions and lacerations of face and body, including
deep cuts on the chin, back, and legs; extensive con-
tusions on chest and trunk; a couple of ribs possibly
fractured. Had he not been so badly hurt, he might
have been at Asano Park, assisting the wounded.

By NIGHTFALL, ten thousand victims of the explosion
had invaded the Red Cross Hospital, and Dr. Sasaki,
worn out, was moving aimlessly and dully up and down
the stinking corridors with wads of bandage and bottles
of Mercurochrome, still wearing the glasses he had

taken from the wounded nurse, binding up the worst cuts as he came to them. Other doctors were putting compresses of saline solution on the worst burns. That was all they could do. After dark, they worked by the light of the city's fires and by candles the ten remaining nurses held for them. Dr. Sasaki had not looked outside the hospital all day; the scene inside was so terrible and so compelling that it had not occurred to him to ask any questions about what had happened beyond the windows and doors. Ceilings and partitions had fallen; plaster, dust, blood, and vomit were everywhere. Patients were dying by the hundreds, but there was nobody to carry away the corpses. Some of the hospital staff distributed biscuits and rice balls, but the charnel-house smell was so strong that few were hungry. By three o'clock the next morning, after nineteen straight hours of his gruesome work, Dr. Sasaki was incapable of dressing another wound. He and some other survivors of the hospital staff got straw mats and went outdoors—thousands of patients and hundreds of dead were in the yard and on the driveway—and hurried around behind the hospital and lay down in hiding to snatch some sleep. But within an hour wounded people had found them; a complaining circle formed around them: "Doctors! Help us! How can you sleep?" Dr. Sasaki got up again and went back to work. Early in the day, he thought for the first time of his mother, at their country home in Mukaihara, thirty miles from town. He usually went home every night. He was afraid she would think he was dead.

Details Are Being Investigated

Near the spot upriver to which Mr. Tanimoto had transported the priests, there sat a large case of rice cakes which a rescue party had evidently brought for the wounded lying thereabouts but hadn't distributed. Before evacuating the wounded priests, the others passed the cakes around and helped themselves. A few minutes later, a band of soldiers came up, and an officer, hearing the priests speaking a foreign language, drew his sword and hysterically asked who they were. One of the priests calmed him down and explained that they were Germans—allies. The officer apologized and said that there were reports going around that American parachutists had landed.

The priests decided that they should take Father Schiffer first. As they prepared to leave, Father Superior LaSalle said he felt awfully cold. One of the Jesuits gave up his coat, another his shirt; they were glad to wear less in the muggy night. The stretcher-bearers started out.. The theological student led the way and tried to warn the others of obstacles, but one of the priests got a foot tangled in some telephone wire and tripped and dropped his corner of the litter. Father Schiffer rolled off, lost consciousness, came to, and then vomited. The bearers picked him up and went on with him to the edge of the city, where they had arranged to meet a relay of other priests, left him with them, and turned back and got the Father Superior.

The wooden litter must have been terribly painful for Father LaSalle, in whose back scores of tiny particles of window glass were embedded. Near the edge of town, the group had to walk around an automobile burned and squatting on the narrow road, and the bearers on one side, unable to see their way in the darkness, fell into a deep ditch. Father LaSalle was thrown onto the ground and the litter broke in two. One priest went ahead to get a handcart from the Novitiate, but he soon found one beside an empty house and wheeled it back. The priests lifted Father LaSalle into the cart and pushed him over the bumpy road the rest of the way. The rector of the Novitiate, who had been a doctor before he entered the religious order, cleaned the wounds of the two priests and put them to bed between clean sheets, and they thanked God for the care they had received.

THOUSANDS of people had nobody to help them. Miss Sasaki was one of them. Abandoned and helpless, under the crude lean-to in the courtyard of the tin factory, beside the woman who had lost a breast and the man whose burned face was scarcely a face any more, she suffered awfully that night from the pain in her broken leg. She did not sleep at all; neither did she converse with her sleepless companions.

IN THE PARK, Mrs. Murata kept Father Kleinsorge awake all night by talking to him. None of the Nakamura family were able to sleep, either; the children, in spite of being very sick, were interested in everything that happened. They were delighted when one of the city's gas-storage tanks went up in a tremendous burst of flame. Toshio, the boy, shouted to the others to look at the reflection in the river. Mr. Tanimoto, after his long run and his many hours of rescue work, dozed uneasily. When he awoke, in the first light of dawn, he looked across the river and saw that he had not carried the festered, limp bodies high enough on the sandspit the night before. The tide had risen above where he had put them; they had not had the strength to move; they must have drowned. He saw a number of bodies floating in the river.

EARLY THAT day, August 7th, the Japanese radio broadcast for the first time a succinct announcement that very few, if any, of the people most concerned with its content, the survivors in Hiroshima, happened to hear: "Hiroshima suffered considerable damage as the result of an attack by a few B-29s. It is believed that a new type of bomb was used. The details are being investigated." Nor is it probable that any of the survivors happened to be tuned in on a shortwave rebroadcast of an extraordinary announcement by the President of the United States, which identified the new bomb as atomic: "That bomb had more power than twenty thousand tons of TNT. It had more than two thousand times the blast power of the British Grand Slam, which is the largest bomb ever yet used in the history of warfare." Those victims who were able to worry at all about what had happened thought of it and discussed it in more primitive, childish terms—gasoline sprinkled from an airplane, maybe, or some combustible gas, or a big cluster of incendiaries, or the work of parachutists; but, even if they had known the truth, most of them were too busy or too weary or too badly hurt to care that they were the objects of the first great experiment in the use of atomic power, which (as the voices on the short-wave shouted) no country except the United States, with its industrial know-how, its willingness to throw two billion gold dollars into an important wartime gamble, could possibly have developed.

Mr. Tanimoto was still angry at doctors. He decided that he would personally bring one to Asano Park—by the scruff of the neck, if necessary. He crossed the river, went past the Shinto shrine where he had met his wife for a brief moment the day before, and walked to the East Parade Ground. Since this had long before been designated as an evacuation area, he thought he would find an aid station there. He did find one, operated by an Army medical unit, but he also saw that its doctors were hopelessly overburdened, with thousands of patients sprawled among corpses across the field in front of it. Nevertheless, he went up to one of the Army doctors and said, as reproachfully as he could, "Why have you not come to Asano Park? You are badly needed there."

Without even looking up from his work, the doctor said in a tired voice, "This is my station."

"But there are many dying on the riverbank over there."

Details Are Being Investigated

"The first duty," the doctor said, "is to take care of the slightly wounded."

"Why—when there are many who are heavily wounded on the riverbank?"

The doctor moved to another patient. "In an emergency like this," he said, as if he were reciting from a manual, "the first task is to help as many as possible—to save as many lives as possible. There is no hope for the heavily wounded. They will die. We can't bother with them."

"That may be right from a medical standpoint—" Mr. Tanimoto began, but then he looked out across the field, where the many dead lay close and intimate with those who were still living, and he turned away without finishing his sentence, angry now with himself. He didn't know what to do; he had promised some of the dying people in the park that he would bring them medical aid. They might die feeling cheated. He saw a ration stand at one side of the field, and he went to it and begged some rice cakes and biscuits, and he took them back, in lieu of doctors, to the people in the park.

THE MORNING, again, was hot. Father Kleinsorge went to fetch water for the wounded in a bottle and a teapot he had borrowed. He had heard that it was possible to get fresh tap water outside Asano Park. Going through the rock gardens, he had to climb over and crawl under the trunks of fallen pine trees; he found he was weak. There were many dead in the gardens. At a beautiful moon bridge, he passed a naked, living woman who seemed to have been burned from head to toe and was red all over. Near the entrance to the park, an Army doctor was working, but the only medicine he had was iodine, which he painted over cuts, bruises, slimy burns, everything—and by now everything that he painted had pus on it. Outside the gate of the park, Father Kleinsorge found a faucet that still worked— part of the plumbing of a vanished house—and he filled his vessels and returned. When he had given the wounded the water, he made a second trip. This time the woman by the bridge was dead. On his way back with the water, he got lost on a detour around a fallen tree, and as he looked for his way through the woods, he heard a voice ask from the underbrush, "Have you anything to drink?" He saw a uniform. Thinking there was just one soldier, he approached with the water. When he had penetrated the bushes, he saw there were about twenty men, and they were all in exactly the same nightmarish state: their faces were wholly burned, their eyesockets were hollow, the fluid from their melted eyes had run down their cheeks. (They must have had their faces upturned when the bomb went off; perhaps they were anti-aircraft personnel.) Their mouths were mere swollen, pus-covered wounds, which they could not bear to stretch enough to admit the spout of the teapot. So Father Kleinsorge got a large piece of grass and drew out the stem so as to make a straw, and gave them all water to drink that way. One of them said, "I can't see anything." Father Kleinsorge answered, as cheerfully as he could, "There's a doctor at the entrance to the park. He's busy now, but he'll come soon and fix your eyes, I hope."

Since that day, Father Kleinsorge has thought back to how queasy he had once been at the sight of pain, how someone else's cut finger used to make him turn faint. Yet there in the park he was so benumbed that immediately after leaving this horrible sight he stopped on a path by one of the pools and discussed with a lightly wounded man whether it would be safe to eat the fat, two-foot carp that floated dead on the surface of the water. They decided, after some consideration, that it would be unwise.

Father Kleinsorge filled the containers a third time and went back to the riverbank. There, amid the dead and dying, he saw a young woman with a needle and thread mending her kimono, which had been slightly torn. Father Kleinsorge joshed her. "My, but you're a dandy!" he said. She laughed.

He felt tired and lay down. He began to talk with two engaging children whose acquaintance he had made the afternoon before. He learned that their name was Kataoka; the girl was thirteen, the boy five. The girl had been just about to set out for a barbershop when the bomb fell. As the family started for Asano Park, their mother decided to turn back for some food and extra clothing; they became separated from her in the crowd of fleeing people, and they had not seen her since. Occasionally they stopped suddenly in their perfectly cheerful playing and began to cry for their mother.

It was difficult for all the children in the park to sustain the sense of tragedy. Toshio Nakamura got quite excited when he saw his friend Seichi Sato riding up the river in a boat with his family, and he ran to the bank and waved and shouted, "Sato! Sato!"

The boy turned his head and shouted, "Who's that?"

"Nakamura."

"Hello, Toshio!"

"Are you all safe?"

"Yes. What about you?"

"Yes, we're all right. My sisters are vomiting, but I'm fine."

Father Kleinsorge began to be thirsty in the dreadful heat, and he did not feel strong enough to go for water again. A little before noon, he saw a Japanese woman handing something out. Soon she came to him and said in a kindly voice, "These are tea leaves. Chew them, young man, and you won't feel thirsty." The woman's gentleness made Father Kleinsorge suddenly want to cry. For weeks, he had been feeling oppressed by the hatred of foreigners that the Japanese seemed increasingly to show, and he had been uneasy even with his Japanese friends. This stranger's gesture made him a little hysterical.

Around noon, the priests arrived from the Novitiate with the handcart. They had been to the site of the mission house in the city and had retrieved some suitcases that had been stored in the air-raid shelter and had also picked up the remains of melted holy vessels in the ashes of the chapel. They now packed Father Kleinsorge's papier-mâché suitcase and the things belonging to Mrs. Murata and the Nakamuras into the cart, put the two Nakamura girls aboard, and prepared to start out. Then one of the Jesuits who had a practical turn of mind remembered that they had been notified some time before that if they suffered property damage at the hands of the enemy, they could enter a claim for compensation with the prefectural police. The holy men discussed this matter there in the park, with the wounded as silent as the dead around them, and decided that Father Kleinsorge, as a former resident of the destroyed mission, was the one to enter the claim. So, as the others went off with the handcart, Father Kleinsorge said goodbye to the Kataoka children and trudged to a police station. Fresh, clean-uniformed policemen from another town were in charge, and a crowd of dirty and disarrayed citizens crowded around them, mostly asking after lost relatives. Father Kleinsorge filled out a claim form and started walking through the center of the town on his way to Nagatsuka. It was then that he first realized the extent of the damage; he passed block after block of ruins, and even after all he had seen in the park, his breath was taken away. By the time he reached the Novitiate, he was sick with exhaustion. The last thing he did as he fell into bed was request that someone go back for the motherless Kataoka children.

ALTOGETHER, Miss Sasaki was left two days and two nights under the piece of propped-up roofing with her crushed leg and her two unpleasant comrades. Her only diversion was when men came to the factory air-raid shelters, which she could see from under one corner of her shelter, and hauled corpses up out of them with ropes. Her leg became discolored, swollen, and putrid. All that time, she went without food and water. On the third day, August 8th, some friends who supposed she was dead came to look for her body and found her. They told her that her mother, father, and baby brother, who at the time of the explosion were in the Tamura Pediatric Hospital, where the baby was a patient, had all been given up as certainly dead, since the hospital was totally destroyed. Her friends then left her to think that piece of news over. Later, some men picked her up by the arms and legs and carried her quite a distance to a truck. For about an hour, the truck moved over a bumpy road, and Miss Sasaki, who had become convinced that she was dulled to pain, discovered that she was not. The men lifted her out at a relief station in the section of Inokuchi, where two Army doctors looked at her. The moment one of them touched her wound, she fainted. She came to in time to hear them discuss whether or not to cut off her leg; one said there was gas gangrene in the lips of the wound and predicted she would die unless they amputated, and the other said that was too bad, because they had no equipment with which to do the job. She fainted again. When she recovered consciousness, she was being carried somewhere on a stretcher. She was put aboard a launch, which went to the nearby island of Ninoshima, and she was taken to a military hospital there. Another doctor examined her and said that she did not have gas gangrene, though she did have a fairly ugly compound fracture. He said quite coldly that he was sorry, but this was a hospital for operative surgical cases only, and because she had no gangrene, she would have to return to Hiroshima that night. But then the doctor took her temperature, and what he saw on the thermometer made him decide to let her stay.

That day, August 8th, Father Cieslik went into the city to look for Mr. Fukai, the Japanese secretary of the diocese, who had ridden unwillingly out of the flaming city on Father Kleinsorge's back and then had run back crazily into it. Father Cieslik started hunting in the neighborhood of Sakai Bridge, where the Jesuits had last seen Mr. Fukai; he went to the East Parade Ground, the evacuation area to which the secretary might have gone, and looked for him among the wounded and dead there; he went to the prefectural police and made inquiries. He could not find any trace of the man. Back at the Novitiate that evening, the theological student, who had been rooming with Mr. Fukai at the mission house, told the priests that the secretary had remarked to him, during an air-raid alarm one day not long before the bombing, "Japan is dying. If there is a real air raid here in Hiroshima, I want to die with our country." The priests concluded that Mr. Fukai had run back to immolate himself in the flames. They never saw him again.

At the Red Cross Hospital, Dr. Sasaki worked for three straight days with only one hour's sleep. On the second day, he began to sew up the worst cuts, and right through the following night and all the next day he stitched. Many of the wounds were festered. Fortunately, someone had found intact a supply of *narucopon*, a Japanese sedative, and he gave it to many who were in pain. Word went around among the staff that there must have been something peculiar about the great bomb, because on the second day the vice-chief of the hospital went down in the basement to the vault where the X-ray plates were stored and found the whole stock exposed as they lay. That day, a fresh doctor and ten nurses came in from the city of Yamaguchi with extra bandages and antiseptics, and the third day another physician and a dozen more nurses arrived from Matsue—yet there were still only eight doctors for ten thousand patients. In the afternoon of the third day, exhausted from his foul tailoring, Dr. Sasaki became obsessed with the idea that his mother thought he was dead. He got permission to go to Mukaihara. He walked out to the first suburbs, beyond which the electric train service was still functioning, and reached home late in the evening. His mother said she had known he was all right all along; a wounded nurse had stopped by to tell her. He went to bed and slept for seventeen hours.

Details Are Being Investigated

BEFORE DAWN on August 8th, someone entered the room at the Novitiate where Father Kleinsorge was in bed, reached up to the hanging light bulb, and switched it on. The sudden flood of light, pouring in on Father Kleinsorge's half sleep, brought him leaping out of bed, braced for a new concussion. When he realized what had happened, he laughed confusedly and went back to bed. He stayed there all day.

On August 9th, Father Kleinsorge was still tired. The rector looked at his cuts and said they were not even worth dressing, and if Father Kleinsorge kept them clean, they would heal in three or four days. Father Kleinsorge felt uneasy; he could not yet comprehend what he had been through; as if he were guilty of something awful, he felt he had to go back to the scene of the violence he had experienced. He got up out of bed and walked into the city. He scratched for a while in the ruins of the mission house, but he found nothing. He went to the sites of a couple of schools and asked after people he knew. He looked for some of the city's Japanese Catholics, but he found only fallen houses. He walked back to the Novitiate, stupefied and without any new understanding.

AT TWO minutes after eleven o'clock on the morning of August 9th, the second atomic bomb was dropped, on Nagasaki. It was several days before the survivors of Hiroshima knew they had company, because the Japanese radio and newspapers were being extremely cautious on the subject of the strange weapon.

HIROSHIMA

On August 9th, Mr. Tanimoto was still working in the park. He went to the suburb of Ushida, where his wife was staying with friends, and got a tent which he had stored there before the bombing. He now took it to the park and set it up as a shelter for some of the wounded who could not move or be moved. Whatever he did in the park, he felt he was being watched by the twenty-year-old girl, Mrs. Kamai, his former neighbor, whom he had seen on the day the bomb exploded, with her dead baby daughter in her arms. She kept the small corpse in her arms for four days, even though it began smelling bad on the second day. Once, Mr. Tanimoto sat with her for a while, and she told him that the bomb had buried her under their house with the baby strapped to her back, and that when she had dug herself free, she had discovered that the baby was choking, its mouth full of dirt. With her little finger, she had carefully cleaned out the infant's mouth, and for a time the child had breathed normally and seemed all right; then suddenly it had died. Mrs. Kamai also talked about what a fine man her husband was, and again urged Mr. Tanimoto to search for him. Since Mr. Tanimoto had been all through the city the first day and had seen terribly burned soldiers from Kamai's post, the Chugoku Regional Army Headquarters, everywhere, he knew it would be impossible to find Kamai, even if he were living, but of course he didn't tell her that. Every time she saw Mr. Tanimoto, she asked whether he had found her husband. Once, he tried to suggest that perhaps it was time to cremate the baby, but Mrs. Kamai only held it tighter. He began to keep away from her, but whenever he looked at her, she was staring at him and her eyes asked the same question. He tried to escape her glance by keeping his back turned to her as much as possible.

THE JESUITS took about fifty refugees into the exquisite chapel of the Novitiate. The rector gave them what medical care he could—mostly just the cleaning away of pus. Each of the Nakamuras was provided with a blanket and a mosquito net. Mrs. Nakamura and her younger daughter had no appetite and ate nothing; her son and other daughter ate, and lost, each meal they were offered. On August 10th, a friend, Mrs. Osaki, came to see them and told them that her son Hideo had been burned alive in the factory where he worked. This Hideo had been a kind of hero to Toshio, who had often gone to the plant to watch him run his machine. That night, Toshio woke up screaming. He had dreamed that he had seen Mrs. Osaki coming out of an opening in the ground with her family, and then he saw Hideo at his machine, a big one with a revolving belt, and he himself was standing beside Hideo, and for some reason this was terrifying.

ON AUGUST 10TH, Father Kleinsorge, having heard from someone that Dr. Fujii had been injured and that he had eventually gone to the summer house of a friend of his named Okuma, in the village of Fukawa, asked Father Cieslik if he would go and see how Dr. Fujii was. Father Cieslik went to Misasa station, outside Hiroshima, rode for twenty minutes on an electric train, and then walked for an hour and a half in a terribly hot sun to Mr. Okuma's house, which was beside the Ota River at the foot of a mountain. He found Dr. Fujii sitting in a chair in a kimono, applying compresses to his broken collarbone. The Doctor told Father Cieslik about having lost his glasses and said that his eyes bothered him. He showed the priest huge blue and green stripes where beams had bruised him. He offered the Jesuit first a cigarette and then whiskey, though it was only eleven in the morning. Father Cieslik thought it would please Dr. Fujii if he took a little, so he said yes. A servant brought some Suntory whiskey, and the Jesuit, the Doctor, and the host had a very pleasant chat. Mr. Okuma had lived in Hawaii, and he told some things about Americans. Dr. Fujii talked a bit about the disaster. He said that Mr. Okuma and a nurse had gone into the ruins of his hospital and brought back a small safe which he had moved into his air-raid shelter. This contained some surgical instruments, and Dr. Fujii gave Father Cieslik a few pairs of scissors and tweezers for the rector at the Novitiate. Father Cieslik was bursting with some inside dope he had, but he waited until the conversation turned naturally to the mystery of the bomb. Then he said he knew what kind of bomb it was; he had the secret on the best authority—that of a Japanese newspaperman who had dropped in at the Novitiate. The bomb was not a bomb at all; it was a kind of fine magnesium powder sprayed over the whole city by a single plane, and it exploded when it came into contact with the live wires of the city power system. "That means," said Dr. Fujii, perfectly satisfied, since after all the information came from a newspaperman, "that it can only be dropped on big cities and only in the daytime, when the tram lines and so forth are in operation."

AFTER FIVE days of ministering to the wounded in the park, Mr. Tanimoto returned, on August 11th, to his parsonage and dug around in the ruins. He retrieved some diaries and church records that had been kept in books and were only charred around the edges, as well as some cooking utensils and pottery. While he was at work, a Miss Tanaka came and said that her father had been asking for him. Mr. Tanimoto had reason to hate her father, the retired shipping-company official who, though he made a great show of his charity, was notoriously selfish and cruel, and who, just a few days before the bombing, had said openly to several people that Mr. Tanimoto was a spy for the Americans. Several times he had derided Christianity and called it un-Japanese. At the moment of the bombing, Mr. Tanaka had been walking in the street in front of the city's radio station. He received serious flash burns, but he was able to walk home. He took refuge in his Neighborhood Association shelter and from there tried hard to get medical aid. He expected all the doctors of Hiroshima to come to him, because he was so rich and so famous for giving his money away. When none of them came, he angrily set out to look for them; leaning on his daughter's arm, he walked from private hospital to private hospital, but all were in ruins, and he went back and lay down in the shelter again. Now he was very weak and knew he was going to die. He was willing to be comforted by any religion.

Mr. Tanimoto went to help him. He descended into the tomblike shelter and, when his eyes were adjusted to the darkness, saw Mr. Tanaka, his face and arms puffed up and covered with pus and blood, and his eyes swollen shut. The old man smelled very bad, and he moaned constantly. He seemed to recognize Mr. Tanimoto's voice. Standing at the shelter stairway to get light, Mr. Tanimoto read loudly from a Japanese-language pocket Bible: "For a thousand years in Thy sight are but as yesterday when it is past, and as a watch in the night. Thou carriest the children of men away as with a flood; they are as a sleep; in the morning they are like grass which groweth up. In the morning it flourisheth and groweth up; in the evening it is cut down, and withereth. For we are consumed by Thine anger and by Thy wrath are we troubled. Thou hast set our iniquities before Thee, our secret sins in the light of Thy countenance. For all our days are passed away in Thy wrath: we spend our years as a tale that is told...."

Mr. Tanaka died as Mr. Tanimoto read the psalm.

Details Are Being Investigated

ON AUGUST 11TH, word came to the Ninoshima Military Hospital that a large number of military casualties from the Chugoku Regional Army Headquarters were to arrive on the island that day, and it was deemed necessary to evacuate all civilian patients. Miss Sasaki, still running an alarmingly high fever, was put on a large ship. She lay out on deck, with a pillow under her leg. There were awnings over the deck, but the vessel's course put her in the sunlight. She felt as if she were under a magnifying glass in the sun. Pus oozed out of her wound, and soon the whole pillow was covered with it. She was taken ashore at Hatsukaichi, a town several miles to the southwest of Hiroshima, and put in the Goddess of Mercy Primary School, which had been turned into a hospital. She lay there for several days before a specialist on fractures came from Kobe. By then her leg was red and swollen up to her hip. The doctor decided he could not set the breaks. He made an incision and put in a rubber pipe to drain off the putrescence.

AT THE Novitiate, the motherless Kataoka children were inconsolable. Father Cieslik worked hard to keep them distracted. He put riddles to them. He asked, "What is the cleverest animal in the world?," and after the thirteen-year-old girl had guessed the ape, the elephant, the horse, he said, "No, it must be the hippopotamus," because in Japanese that animal is *kaba*, the reverse of *baka*, stupid. He told Bible stories, beginning, in the order of things, with the Creation. He showed them a scrapbook of snapshots taken in Europe. Nevertheless, they cried most of the time for their mother.

Several days later, Father Cieslik started hunting for the children's family. First, he learned through the police that an uncle had been to the authorities in Kure, a city not far away, to inquire for the children. After that, he heard that an older brother had been trying to trace them through the post office in Ujina, a suburb of Hiroshima. Still later, he heard that the mother was alive and was on Goto Island, off Nagasaki. And at last, by keeping a check on the Ujina post office, he got in touch with the brother and returned the children to their mother.

ABOUT a week after the bomb dropped, a vague, incomprehensible rumor reached Hiroshima—that the city had been destroyed by the energy released when atoms were somehow split in two. The weapon was referred to in this word-of-mouth report as *genshi bakudan*—the root characters of which can be translated as "original child bomb." No one understood the idea or put any more credence in it than in the powdered magnesium and such things. Newspapers were being brought in from other cities, but they were still confining themselves to extremely general statements, such as Domei's assertion on August 12th: "There is nothing to do but admit the tremendous power of this inhuman bomb." Already, Japanese physicists had entered the city with Lauritsen electroscopes and Neher electrometers; they understood the idea all too well.

ON AUGUST 12TH, the Nakamuras, all of them still rather sick, went to the nearby town of Kabe and moved in with Mrs. Nakamura's sister-in-law. The next day, Mrs. Nakamura, although she was too ill to walk much, returned to Hiroshima alone, by electric car to the outskirts, by foot from there. All week, at the Novitiate, she had worried about her mother, brother, and older sister, who had lived in the part of town called Fukuro, and besides, she felt drawn by some fascination, just as Father Kleinsorge had been. She discovered that her family were all dead. She went back to Kabe so amazed and depressed by what she had seen and learned in the city that she could not speak that evening.

A COMPARATIVE orderliness, at least, began to be established at the Red Cross Hospital. Dr. Sasaki, back from his rest, undertook to classify his patients (who were still scattered everywhere, even on the stairways). The staff gradually swept up the debris. Best of all, the nurses and attendants started to remove the corpses. Disposal of the dead, by decent cremation and enshrinement, is a greater moral responsibility to the Japanese than adequate care of the living. Relatives identified most of the first day's dead in and around the hospital. Beginning on the second day, whenever a patient appeared to be moribund, a piece of paper with his name on it was fastened to his clothing. The corpse detail carried the bodies to a clearing outside, placed them on pyres of wood from ruined houses, burned them, put some of the ashes in envelopes intended for exposed X-ray plates, marked the envelopes with the names of the deceased, and piled them, neatly and respectfully, in stacks in the main office. In a few days, the envelopes filled one whole side of the impromptu shrine.

In Kabe, on the morning of August 15th, ten-year-old Toshio Nakamura heard an airplane overhead. He ran outdoors and identified it with a professional eye as a B-29. "There goes Mr. B!" he shouted.

One of his relatives called out to him, "Haven't you had enough of Mr. B?"

The question had a kind of symbolism. At almost that very moment, the dull, dispirited voice of Hirohito, the Emperor Tenno, was speaking for the first time in history over the radio: "After pondering deeply the general trends of the world and the actual conditions obtaining in Our Empire today, We have decided to effect a settlement of the present situation by resorting to an extraordinary measure. . . ."

Mrs. Nakamura had gone to the city again, to dig up some rice she had buried in her Neighborhood Association air-raid shelter. She got it and started back for Kabe. On the electric car, quite by chance, she ran into her younger sister, who had not been in Hiroshima the day of the bombing. "Have you heard the news?" her sister asked.

"What news?"

"The war is over."

"Don't say such a foolish thing, sister."

"But I heard it over the radio myself." And then, in a whisper, "It was the Emperor's voice."

"Oh," Mrs. Nakamura said (she needed nothing more to make her give up thinking, in spite of the atomic bomb, that Japan still had a chance to win the war), "in that case . . ."

SOME time later, in a letter to an American, Mr. Tanimoto described the events of that morning. "At the time of the Post-War, the marvelous thing in our history happened. Our Emperor broadcasted his own voice through radio directly to us, common people of Japan. Aug. 15th we were told that some news of great importance could be heard & all of us should hear it. So I went to Hiroshima railway station. There set a loud-speaker in the ruins of the station. Many civilians, all of them were in boundage, some being helped by shoulder of their daughters, some sustaining their injured feet by sticks, they listened to the broadcast and when they came to realize the fact that it was the Emperor, they cried with full tears in their eyes, 'What a wonderful blessing it is that Tenno himself call on us and we can hear his own voice in person. We are thoroughly satisfied in such a great sacrifice.' When they came to know the war was ended—that is, Japan was defeated, they, of course, were deeply disappointed, but followed after their Emperor's commandment in calm spirit, making whole-hearted sacrifice for the everlasting peace of the world—and Japan started her new way."

IV · *Panic Grass and Feverfew*

O N AUGUST 18TH, twelve days after the bomb burst, Father Kleinsorge set out on foot for Hiroshima from the Novitiate with his papier-mâché suitcase in his hand. He had begun to think that this bag, in which he kept his valuables, had a talismanic quality, because of the way he had found it after the explosion, standing handle-side up in the doorway of his room, while the desk under which he had previously hidden it was in splinters all over the floor. Now he was using it to carry the yen belonging to the Society of Jesus to the Hiroshima branch of the Yokohama Specie Bank, already reopened in its half-ruined building. On the whole, he felt quite well that morning. It is true that the minor cuts he had received had not healed in three or four days, as the rector of the Novitiate, who had examined them, had positively promised they would, but Father Kleinsorge had rested well for a week and considered that he was again ready for hard work. By now he was accustomed to the terrible scene through which he walked on his way into the city: the large rice field near the Novitiate, streaked with brown; the houses on the outskirts of the city, standing but decrepit, with broken windows and dishevelled tiles; and then, quite suddenly, the beginning of the four square miles of reddish-brown scar, where nearly everything had been buffeted down and burned; range on range of collapsed city blocks, with here and there a crude sign erected on a pile of ashes and tiles ("Sister, where are you?" or "All safe and we live at Toyosaka"); naked trees and canted telephone poles; the few standing, gutted buildings only accentuating the horizontality of everything else (the Museum of Science and Industry, with its dome stripped to its steel frame, as if for an autopsy; the modern Chamber of Commerce Building, its tower as cold, rigid, and unassailable after the blow as before; the huge, low-lying, camouflaged city hall; the row of dowdy banks, caricaturing a shaken economic system); and in the streets a macabre traffic —hundreds of crumpled bicycles, shells of streetcars and automobiles, all halted in mid-motion. The whole way, Father Kleinsorge was oppressed by the thought that all the damage he saw had been done in one instant by one bomb. By the time he reached the center of town, the day had become very hot. He walked to the Yokohama Bank, which was doing business in a temporary wooden stall on the ground floor of its building, deposited the money, went by the mission compound just to have another look at the wreckage,

and then started back to the Novitiate. About halfway
there, he began to have peculiar sensations. The more
or less magical suitcase, now empty, suddenly seemed
terribly heavy. His knees grew weak. He felt excruciatingly tired. With a considerable expenditure of spirit,
he managed to reach the Novitiate. He did not think
his weakness was worth mentioning to the other Jesuits.
But a couple of days later, while attempting to say
Mass, he had an onset of faintness and even after three
attempts was unable to go through with the service,
and the next morning the rector, who had examined
Father Kleinsorge's apparently negligible but un-
healed cuts daily, asked in surprise, "What have you
done to your wounds?" They had suddenly opened
wider and were swollen and inflamed.

As she dressed on the morning of August 20th, in
the home of her sister-in-law in Kabe, not far from
Nagatsuka, Mrs. Nakamura, who had suffered no cuts
or burns at all, though she had been rather nauseated
all through the week she and her children had spent
as guests of Father Kleinsorge and the other Catholics
at the Novitiate, began fixing her hair and noticed,
after one stroke, that her comb carried with it a whole
handful of hair; the second time, the same thing happened, so she stopped combing at once. But in the next
three or four days, her hair kept falling out of its own
accord, until she was quite bald. She began living indoors, practically in hiding. On August 26th, both she
and her younger daughter, Myeko, woke up feeling
extremely weak and tired, and they stayed on their

bedrolls. Her son and other daughter, who had shared every experience with her during and after the bombing, felt fine.

At about the same time—he lost track of the days, so hard was he working to set up a temporary place of worship in a private house he had rented in the outskirts—Mr. Tanimoto fell suddenly ill with a general malaise, weariness, and feverishness, and he, too, took to his bedroll on the floor of the half-wrecked house of a friend in the suburb of Ushida.

These four did not realize it, but they were coming down with the strange, capricious disease which came later to be known as radiation sickness.

MISS SASAKI lay in steady pain in the Goddess of Mercy Primary School, at Hatsukaichi, the fourth station to the southwest of Hiroshima on the electric train. An internal infection still prevented the proper setting of the compound fracture of her lower left leg. A young man who was in the same hospital and who seemed to have grown fond of her in spite of her unremitting preoccupation with her suffering, or else just pitied her because of it, lent her a Japanese translation of de Maupassant, and she tried to read the stories, but she could concentrate for only four or five minutes at a time.

The hospitals and aid stations around Hiroshima were so crowded in the first weeks after the bombing, and their staffs were so variable, depending on their health and on the unpredictable arrival of outside help, that patients had to be constantly shifted from place to place. Miss Sasaki, who had already been moved three times, twice by ship, was taken at the end of August to an engineering school, also at Hatsukaichi. Because her leg did not improve but swelled more and more, the doctors at the school bound it with crude splints and took her by car, on September 9th, to the Red Cross Hospital in Hiroshima. This was the first chance she had had to look at the ruins of Hiroshima; the last time she had been carried through the city's streets, she had been hovering on the edge of unconsciousness. Even though the wreckage had been described to her, and though she was still in pain, the sight horrified and amazed her, and there was something she noticed about it that particularly gave her the creeps. Over everything—up through the wreckage of the city, in gutters, along the riverbanks, tangled among tiles and tin roofing, climbing on charred tree trunks—was a blanket of fresh, vivid, lush, optimistic green; the verdancy rose even from the foundations of ruined houses. Weeds already hid the ashes, and wild flowers were in bloom among the city's bones. The bomb had not only left the underground organs of plants intact; it had stimulated them. Everywhere were bluets and Spanish bayonets, goosefoot, morning glories and day lilies, the hairy-fruited bean, purslane and clotbur and sesame and panic grass and feverfew. Especially in a circle at the center, sickle senna grew in extraordinary regeneration, not only standing among the charred remnants of the same plant but pushing up in new places, among bricks and through cracks in the asphalt. It actually seemed as if a load of sickle-senna seed had been dropped along with the bomb.

At the Red Cross Hospital, Miss Sasaki was put under the care of Dr. Sasaki. Now, a month after the explosion, something like order had been reëstablished in the hospital; which is to say that the patients who still lay in the corridors at least had mats to sleep on and that the supply of medicines, which had given out in the first few days, had been replaced, though inadequately, by contributions from other cities. Dr. Sasaki, who had had one seventeen-hour sleep at his home on the third night, had ever since then rested only about six hours a night, on a mat at the hospital; he had lost twenty pounds from his very small body; he still wore the borrowed glasses.

Since Miss Sasaki was a woman and was so sick (and perhaps, he afterward admitted, just a little bit because she was named Sasaki), Dr. Sasaki put her on a mat in a semi-private room, which at that time had only eight people in it. He questioned her and put down on her record card, in the correct, scrunched-up German in which he wrote all his records: *"Mittelgrosse Patientin in gutem Ernährungszustand. Fraktur am linken Unterschenkelknochen mit Wunde; Anschwellung in der linken Unterschenkelgegend. Haut und sichtbare Schleimhäute mässig durchblutet und kein Oedema,"* noting that she was a medium-sized female patient in good general health; that she had a compound fracture of the left tibia, with swelling of the left lower leg; that her skin and visible mucous membranes were heavily spotted with *petechiae*, which are hemorrhages about the size of grains of rice, or even as big as soybeans; and, in addition, that her head, eyes, throat, lungs, and heart were apparently normal; and that she had a fever. He wanted to set her fracture and put her leg in a cast, but he had run out of plaster of Paris long since, so he just stretched her out on a mat and prescribed aspirin for her fever, and glucose intravenously and diastase orally for her undernourishment (which he had not entered on her record because everyone suffered from it). She exhibited only one of the queer symptoms so many of his patients were just then beginning to show—the spot hemorrhages.

DR. FUJII was still pursued by bad luck, which still was connected with rivers. Now he was living in the summer house of Mr. Okuma, in Fukawa. This house clung to the steep banks of the Ota River. Here his injuries seemed to make good progress, and he even began to treat refugees who came to him from the neighborhood, using medical supplies he had retrieved from a cache in the suburbs. He noticed in some of his patients a curious syndrome of symptoms that cropped out in the third and fourth weeks, but he was not able to do much more than swathe cuts and burns. Early in September, it began to rain, steadily and heavily. The river rose. On September 17th, there came a cloudburst and then a typhoon, and the water crept higher and higher up the bank. Mr. Okuma and Dr. Fujii became alarmed and scrambled up the mountain to a peasant's house. (Down in Hiroshima, the flood took up where the bomb had left off—swept away bridges that had survived the blast, washed out streets, undermined foundations of buildings that still stood—and ten miles to the west, the Ono Army Hospital, where a team of experts from Kyoto Imperial University was studying the delayed affliction of the patients, suddenly slid down a beautiful, pine-dark mountainside into the Inland Sea and drowned most of the investigators and their mysteriously diseased patients alike.) After the storm, Dr. Fujii and Mr. Okuma went down to the river and found that the Okuma house had been washed altogether away.

BECAUSE so many people were suddenly feeling sick nearly a month after the atomic bomb was dropped, an unpleasant rumor began to move around, and eventually it made its way to the house in Kabe where Mrs. Nakamura lay bald and ill. It was that the atomic bomb had deposited some sort of poison on Hiroshima which would give off deadly emanations for seven years; nobody could go there all that time. This especially upset Mrs. Nakamura, who remembered that in a moment of confusion on the morning of the explosion she had literally sunk her entire means of livelihood, her Sankoku sewing machine, in the small cement water tank in front of what was left of her house; now no one would be able to go and fish it out. Up to this time, Mrs. Nakamura and her relatives had been quite resigned and passive about the moral issue of the atomic bomb, but this rumor suddenly aroused them to more hatred and resentment of America than they had felt all through the war.

Japanese physicists, who knew a great deal about atomic fission (one of them owned a cyclotron), worried about lingering radiation at Hiroshima, and in mid-August, not many days after President Truman's disclosure of the type of bomb that had been dropped, they entered the city to make investigations. The first thing they did was roughly to determine a center by observing the side on which telephone poles all around the heart of the town were scorched; they settled on the torii gateway of the Gokoku Shrine, right next to the parade ground of the Chugoku Regional Army Headquarters. From there, they worked north and south with Lauritsen electroscopes, which are sensitive to both beta particles and gamma rays. These indicated that the highest intensity of radioactivity, near the torii, was 4.2 times the average natural "leak" of ultra-short waves for the earth of that area. The scientists noticed that the flash of the bomb had discolored concrete to a light reddish tint, had scaled off the surface of granite, and had scorched certain other types of building material, and that consequently the bomb had, in some places, left prints of the shadows that had been cast by its light. The experts found, for instance, a permanent shadow thrown on the roof of the Chamber of Commerce Building (220 yards from the rough center) by the structure's rectangular tower; several others in the lookout post on top of the Hypothec Bank (2,050 yards); another in the tower of the Chugoku Electric Supply Building (800 yards); another projected by the handle of a gas pump (2,630 yards); and several on granite tombstones in the Gokoku Shrine (385 yards). By triangulating these and other such shadows with the objects that formed them, the scientists determined that the exact center was a spot a hundred and fifty yards south of the torii and a few yards southeast of the pile of ruins that had once been the Shima Hospital. (A few vague human silhouettes were found, and these gave rise to stories that eventually included fancy and precise details. One story told how a painter on a ladder was monumentalized in a kind of bas-relief on the stone façade of a bank building on which he was at work, in the act of dipping his brush into his paint can; another, how a man and his cart on the bridge near the Museum of Science and Industry, almost under the center of the explosion, were cast down in an embossed shadow which made it clear that the man was about to whip his horse.) Starting east and west from the actual center, the scientists, in early September, made new measurements, and the highest radiation they found this time was 3.9 times the natural "leak." Since radiation of at least a thousand times the natural "leak" would be required to cause serious effects on the human body, the scientists announced that people could enter Hiroshima without any peril at all.

As soon as this reassurance reached the household in which Mrs. Nakamura was concealing herself—or, at any rate, within a short time, after her hair had started growing back again—her whole family relaxed their extreme hatred of America, and Mrs. Nakamura sent her brother-in-law to look for the sewing machine. It was still submerged in the water tank, and when he brought it home, she saw, to her dismay, that it was all rusted and useless.

By the end of the first week in September, Father Kleinsorge was in bed at the Novitiate with a fever of 102.2, and since he seemed to be getting worse, his colleagues decided to send him to the Catholic International Hospital in Tokyo. Father Cieslik and the rector took him as far as Kobe and a Jesuit from that city took him the rest of the way, with a message from a Kobe doctor to the Mother Superior of the International Hospital: "Think twice before you give this man blood transfusions, because with atomic-bomb patients we aren't at all sure that if you stick needles in them, they'll stop bleeding."

When Father Kleinsorge arrived at the hospital, he was terribly pale and very shaky. He complained that the bomb had upset his digestion and given him abdominal pains. His white blood count was three thousand (five to seven thousand is normal), he was seriously anemic, and his temperature was 104. A doctor who did not know much about these strange manifestations—Father Kleinsorge was one of a handful of atomic patients who had reached Tokyo—came to see him, and to the patient's face he was most encouraging. "You'll be out of here in two weeks," he said. But when the doctor got out in the corridor, he said to the Mother Superior, "He'll die. All these bomb people die—you'll see. They go along for a couple of weeks and then they die."

The doctor prescribed suralimentation for Father Kleinsorge. Every three hours, they forced some eggs or beef juice into him, and they fed him all the sugar he could stand. They gave him vitamins, and iron pills and arsenic (in Fowler's solution) for his anemia. He confounded both the doctor's predictions; he neither died nor got up in a fortnight. Despite the fact that the message from the Kobe doctor deprived him of transfusions, which would have been the most useful therapy of all, his fever and his digestive troubles cleared up fairly quickly. His white count went up for a while, but early in October it dropped again, to 3,600; then, in ten days, it suddenly climbed above normal, to 8,800; and it finally settled at 5,800. His ridiculous scratches puzzled everyone. For a few days, they would mend, and then, when he moved around, they would open up again. As soon as he began to feel well, he enjoyed himself tremendously. In Hiroshima he had been one of thousands of sufferers; in Tokyo he was a curiosity. American Army doctors came by the dozen to observe him. Japanese experts questioned him. A newspaper interviewed him. And once, the confused doctor came and shook his head and said, "Baffling cases, these atomic-bomb people."

MRS. NAKAMURA lay indoors with Myeko. They both continued sick, and though Mrs. Nakamura vaguely sensed that their trouble was caused by the bomb, she was too poor to see a doctor and so never knew exactly what the matter was. Without any treatment at all, but merely resting, they began gradually to feel better. Some of Myeko's hair fell out, and she had a tiny burn on her arm which took months to heal. The boy, Toshio, and the older girl, Yaeko, seemed well enough, though they, too, lost some hair and occasionally had bad headaches. Toshio was still having nightmares, always about the nineteen-year-old mechanic, Hideo Osaki, his hero, who had been killed by the bomb.

ON HIS BACK with a fever of 104, Mr. Tanimoto worried about all the funerals he ought to be conducting for the deceased of his church. He thought he was just overtired from the hard work he had done since the bombing, but after the fever had persisted for a few days, he sent for a doctor. The doctor was too busy to visit him in Ushida, but he dispatched a nurse, who recognized his symptoms as those of mild radiation disease and came back from time to time to give him injections of Vitamin B_1. A Buddhist priest with whom Mr. Tanimoto was acquainted called on him and suggested that moxibustion might give him relief; the priest showed the pastor how to give himself the ancient Japanese treatment, by setting fire to a twist of the stimulant herb moxa placed on the wrist pulse. Mr. Tanimoto found that each moxa treatment temporarily reduced his fever one degree. The nurse had told him to eat as much as possible, and every few days his mother-in-law brought him vegetables and fish from Tsuzu, twenty miles away, where she lived. He spent a month in bed, and then went ten hours by train to his father's home in Shikoku. There he rested another month.

DR. SASAKI and his colleagues at the Red Cross Hospital watched the unprecedented disease unfold and at last evolved a theory about its nature. It had, they decided, three stages. The first stage had been all over before the doctors even knew they were dealing with a new sickness; it was the direct reaction to the bombardment of the body, at the moment when the bomb went off, by neutrons, beta particles, and gamma rays. The apparently uninjured people who had died so mysteriously in the first few hours or days had succumbed in this first stage. It killed ninety-five per cent of the people within a half mile of the center, and many thousands who were farther away. The doctors realized in retrospect that even though most of these dead had also suffered from burns and blast effects, they had absorbed enough radiation to kill them. The rays simply destroyed body cells—caused their nuclei to degenerate and broke their walls. Many people who did not die right away came down with nausea, headache, diarrhea, malaise, and fever, which lasted several days. Doctors could not be certain whether some of these symptoms were the result of radiation or nervous shock. The second stage set in ten or fifteen days after the bombing. Its first symptom was falling hair. Diarrhea and fever, which in some cases went as high as 106, came next. Twenty-five to thirty days after the explosion, blood disorders appeared: gums bled, the white-blood-cell count dropped sharply, and *petechiae* appeared on the skin and mucous membranes. The drop in the number of white blood corpuscles reduced the patient's capacity to resist infection, so open wounds were unusually slow in healing and many of the sick developed sore throats and mouths. The two key symptoms, on which the doctors came to base their prognosis, were fever and the lowered white-corpuscle count. If fever remained steady and high, the patient's chances for survival were poor. The white count almost always dropped below four thousand; a patient whose count fell below one thousand had little hope of living. Toward the end of the second stage, if the patient survived, anemia, or a drop in the red blood count, also set in. The third stage was the reaction that came when the body struggled to compensate for its ills—when, for instance, the white count not only returned to normal but increased to much higher than normal levels. In this stage, many patients died of complications, such as infections in the chest cavity.

Most burns healed with deep layers of pink, rubbery scar tissue, known as keloid tumors. The duration of the disease varied, depending on the patient's constitution and the amount of radiation he had received. Some victims recovered in a week; with others the disease dragged on for months.

As the symptoms revealed themselves, it became clear that many of them resembled the effects of overdoses of X-ray, and the doctors based their therapy on that likeness. They gave victims liver extract, blood transfusions, and vitamins, especially B_1. The shortage of supplies and instruments hampered them. Allied doctors who came in after the surrender found plasma and penicillin very effective. Since the blood disorders were, in the long run, the predominant factor in the disease, some of the Japanese doctors evolved a theory as to the seat of the delayed sickness. They thought that perhaps gamma rays, entering the body at the time of the explosion, made the phosphorus in the victims' bones radioactive, and that they in turn emitted beta particles, which, though they could not penetrate far through flesh, could enter the bone marrow, where blood is manufactured, and gradually tear it down. Whatever its source, the disease had some baffling quirks. Not all the patients exhibited all the main symptoms. People who suffered flash burns were protected, to a considerable extent, from radiation sickness. Those who had lain quietly for days or even hours after the bombing were much less liable to get sick than

those who had been active. Gray hair seldom fell out.
And, as if nature were protecting man against his own
ingenuity, the reproductive processes were affected for
a time; men became sterile, women had miscarriages,
menstruation stopped.

For TEN days after the flood, Dr. Fujii lived in the
peasant's house on the mountain above the Ota. Then
he heard about a vacant private clinic in Kaitaichi, a
suburb to the east of Hiroshima. He bought it at
once, moved there, and hung out a sign inscribed in
English, in honor of the conquerors:

M. FUJII, M.D.
MEDICAL & VENEREAL

Quite recovered from his wounds, he soon built up a
strong practice, and he was delighted, in the evenings,
to receive members of the occupying forces, on whom
he lavished whiskey and practiced English.

GIVING Miss Sasaki a local anaesthetic of procaine, Dr.
Sasaki made an incision in her leg on October 23rd, to
drain the infection, which still lingered on eleven
weeks after the injury. In the following days, so much
pus formed that he had to dress the opening each morning and evening. A week later, she complained of great
pain, so he made another incision; he cut still a third,
on November 9th, and enlarged it on the twenty-sixth.
All this time, Miss Sasaki grew weaker and weaker, and

her spirits fell low. One day, the young man who had lent her his translation of de Maupassant at Hatsu-kaichi came to visit her; he told her that he was going to Kyushu but that when he came back, he would like to see her again. She didn't care. Her leg had been so swollen and painful all along that the doctor had not even tried to set the fractures, and though an X-ray taken in November showed that the bones were mending, she could see under the sheet that her left leg was nearly three inches shorter than her right and that her left foot was turning inward. She thought often of the man to whom she had been engaged. Someone told her he was back from overseas. She wondered what he had heard about her injuries that made him stay away.

FATHER KLEINSORGE was discharged from the hospital in Tokyo on December 19th and took a train home. On the way, two days later, at Yokogawa, a stop just before Hiroshima, Dr. Fujii boarded the train. It was the first time the two men had met since before the bombing. They sat together. Dr. Fujii said he was going to the annual gathering of his family, on the anniversary of his father's death. When they started talking about their experiences, the Doctor was quite entertaining as he told how his places of residence kept falling into rivers. Then he asked Father Kleinsorge how he was, and the Jesuit talked about his stay in the hospital. "The doctors told me to be cautious," he said. "They ordered me to have a two-hour nap every afternoon."

Panic Grass and Feverfew

Dr. Fujii said, "It's hard to be cautious in Hiroshima these days. Everyone seems to be so busy."

A NEW municipal government, set up under Allied Military Government direction, had gone to work at last in the city hall. Citizens who had recovered from various degrees of radiation sickness were coming back by the thousand—by November 1st, the population, mostly crowded into the outskirts, was already 137,000, more than a third of the wartime peak—and the government set in motion all kinds of projects to put them to work rebuilding the city. It hired men to clear the streets, and others to gather scrap iron, which they sorted and piled in mountains opposite the city hall. Some returning residents were putting up their own shanties and huts, and planting small squares of winter wheat beside them, but the city also authorized and built four hundred one-family "barracks." Utilities were repaired—electric lights shone again, trams started running, and employees of the waterworks fixed seventy thousand leaks in mains and plumbing. A Planning Conference, with an enthusiastic young Military Government officer, Lieutenant John D. Montgomery, of Kalamazoo, as its adviser, began to consider what sort of city the new Hiroshima should be. The ruined city had flourished—and had been an inviting target—mainly because it had been one of the most important military-command and communications centers in Japan, and would have become the Imperial headquarters had the islands been invaded and Tokyo been captured. Now there would be no huge military establishments to help revive the city. The Planning Conference, at a loss as to just what importance Hiroshima could have, fell back on rather vague cultural and paving projects. It drew maps with avenues a hundred yards wide and thought seriously of erecting a group of buildings as a monument to the disaster, and naming them the Institute of International Amity. Statistical workers gathered what figures they could on the effects of the bomb. They reported that 78,150 people had been killed, 13,983 were missing, and 37,425 had been injured. No one in the city government pretended that these figures were accurate—though the Americans accepted them as official—and as the months went by and more and more hundreds of corpses were dug up from the ruins, and as the number of unclaimed urns of ashes at the Zempoji Temple in Koi rose into the thousands, the statisticians began to say that at least a hundred thousand people had lost their lives in the bombing. Since many people died of a combination of causes, it was impossible to figure exactly how many were killed by each cause, but the statisticians calculated that about twenty-five per cent had died of direct burns from the bomb, about fifty per cent from other injuries, and about twenty per cent as a result of radiation effects. The statisticians' figures on property damage were more reliable: sixty-two thousand out of ninety thousand buildings destroyed, and six thousand more damaged beyond repair. In the heart of the city, they found only five modern buildings that could be used again

Panic Grass and Feverfew

without major repairs. This small number was by no means the fault of flimsy Japanese construction. In fact, since the 1923 earthquake, Japanese building regulations had required that the roof of each large building be able to bear a minimum load of seventy pounds per square foot, whereas American regulations do not normally specify more than forty pounds per square foot.

Scientists swarmed into the city. Some of them measured the force that had been necessary to shift marble gravestones in the cemeteries, to knock over twenty-two of the forty-seven railroad cars in the yards at Hiroshima station, to lift and move the concrete roadway on one of the bridges, and to perform other noteworthy acts of strength, and concluded that the pressure exerted by the explosion varied from 5.3 to 8.0 tons per square yard. Others found that mica, of which the melting point is 900° C., had fused on granite gravestones three hundred and eighty yards from the center; that telephone poles of *Cryptomeria japonica*, whose carbonization temperature is 240° C., had been charred at forty-four hundred yards from the center; and that the surface of gray clay tiles of the type used in Hiroshima, whose melting point is 1,300° C., had dissolved at six hundred yards; and, after examining other significant ashes and melted bits, they concluded that the bomb's heat on the ground at the center must have been 6,000° C. And from further measurements of radiation, which involved, among other things, the scraping up of fission fragments from roof troughs and drainpipes as far away

107

as the suburb of Takasu, thirty-three hundred yards
from the center, they learned some far more important
facts about the nature of the bomb. General MacArthur's headquarters systematically censored all mention of the bomb in Japanese scientific publications,
but soon the fruit of the scientists' calculations became
common knowledge among Japanese physicists, doctors, chemists, journalists, professors, and, no doubt,
those statesmen and military men who were still in
circulation. Long before the American public had been
told, most of the scientists and lots of non-scientists in
Japan knew—from the calculations of Japanese nuclear
physicists—that a uranium bomb had exploded at Hiroshima and a more powerful one, of plutonium, at Nagasaki. They also knew that theoretically one ten times as
powerful—or twenty—could be developed. The Japanese scientists thought they knew the exact height at
which the bomb at Hiroshima was exploded and the
approximate weight of the uranium used. They estimated that, even with the primitive bomb used at Hiroshima, it would require a shelter of concrete fifty inches
thick to protect a human being entirely from radiation
sickness. The scientists had these and other details
which remained subject to security in the United States
printed and mimeographed and bound into little
books. The Americans knew of the existence of these,
but tracing them and seeing that they did not fall into
the wrong hands would have obliged the occupying authorities to set up, for this one purpose alone,
an enormous police system in Japan. Altogether, the

Japanese scientists were somewhat amused at the efforts of their conquerors to keep security on atomic fission.

LATE IN February, 1946, a friend of Miss Sasaki's called on Father Kleinsorge and asked him to visit her in the hospital. She had been growing more and more depressed and morbid; she seemed little interested in living. Father Kleinsorge went to see her several times. On his first visit, he kept the conversation general, formal, and yet vaguely sympathetic, and did not mention religion. Miss Sasaki herself brought it up the second time he dropped in on her. Evidently she had had some talks with a Catholic. She asked bluntly, "If your God is so good and kind, how can he let people suffer like this?" She made a gesture which took in her shrunken leg, the other patients in her room, and Hiroshima as a whole.

"My child," Father Kleinsorge said, "man is not now in the condition God intended. He has fallen from grace through sin." And he went on to explain all the reasons for everything.

IT CAME to Mrs. Nakamura's attention that a carpenter from Kabe was building a number of wooden shanties in Hiroshima which he rented for fifty yen a month—about fifty cents, at the fixed rate of exchange. Mrs. Nakamura had lost the certificates for her bonds and other wartime savings, but fortunately she had copied off all the numbers just a few days before the bombing and had taken the list to Kabe, and so, when her hair had grown in enough for her to be presentable, she went to her bank in Hiroshima, and a clerk there told her that after checking her numbers against the records the bank would give her her money. As soon as she got it, she rented one of the carpenter's shacks. It was in Nobori-cho, near the site of her former house, and though its floor was dirt and it was dark inside, it was at least a home in Hiroshima, and she was no longer dependent on the charity of her in-laws. During the spring, she cleared away some nearby wreckage and planted a vegetable garden. She cooked with utensils and ate off plates she scavenged from the debris. She sent Myeko to the kindergarten which the Jesuits re-opened, and the two older children attended Nobori-cho Primary School, which, for want of buildings, held classes out of doors. Toshio wanted to study to be a mechanic, like his hero, Hideo Osaki. Prices were high; by midsummer Mrs. Nakamura's savings were gone. She sold some of her clothes to get food. She had once had several expensive kimonos, but during the war one had been stolen, she had given one to a sister who had been bombed out in Tokuyama, she had lost a couple in the Hiroshima bombing, and now she sold her last one. It brought only a hundred yen, which did not last long. In June, she went to Father Kleinsorge for advice about how to get along, and in early August, she was still considering the two alternatives he suggested—taking work as a domestic for some of the Allied occupation forces, or borrowing from her relatives enough money, about five hundred yen, or a bit more than thirty dollars, to repair her rusty sewing machine and resume the work of a seamstress.

WHEN Mr. Tanimoto returned from Shikoku, he draped a tent he owned over the roof of the badly damaged house he had rented in Ushida. The roof still leaked, but he conducted services in the damp living room. He began thinking about raising money to restore his church in the city. He became quite friendly with Father Kleinsorge and saw the Jesuits often. He envied them their Church's wealth; they seemed to be able to do anything they wanted. He had nothing to work with except his own energy, and that was not what it had been.

THE Society of Jesus had been the first institution to build a relatively permanent shanty in the ruins of Hiroshima. That had been while Father Kleinsorge was in the hospital. As soon as he got back, he began living in the shack, and he and another priest, Father Laderman, who had joined him in the mission, arranged for the purchase of three of the standardized "barracks," which the city was selling at seven thousand yen apiece. They put two together, end to end, and made a pretty chapel of them; they ate in the third. When materials were available, they commissioned a contractor to build a three-story mission house exactly like the one that had been destroyed in the fire. In the compound, carpenters cut timbers, gouged mortises, shaped tenons, whittled scores of wooden pegs and bored holes for them, until all the parts for the house were in a neat pile; then, in three days, they put the whole thing together, like an Oriental puzzle, without any nails at all. Father Kleinsorge was finding it hard, as Dr. Fujii had suggested he would, to be cautious and to take his naps. He went out every day on foot to call on Japanese Catholics and prospective converts. As the months went by, he grew more and more tired. In June, he read an article in the Hiroshima *Chugoku* warning survivors against working too hard—but what could he do? By July, he was worn out, and early in August, almost exactly on the anniversary of the bombing, he went back to the Catholic International Hospital, in Tokyo, for a month's rest.

WHETHER or not Father Kleinsorge's answers to Miss Sasaki's questions about life were final and absolute truths, she seemed quickly to draw physical strength from them. Dr. Sasaki noticed it and congratulated Father Kleinsorge. By April 15th, her temperature and white count were normal and the infection in the wound was beginning to clear up. On the twentieth, there was almost no pus, and for the first time she jerked along a corridor on crutches. Five days later, the wound had begun to heal, and on the last day of the month she was discharged.

During the early summer, she prepared herself for conversion to Catholicism. In that period she had ups and downs. Her depressions were deep. She knew she would always be a cripple. Her fiancé never came to see her. There was nothing for her to do except read and look out, from her house on a hillside in Koi, across the ruins of the city where her parents and brother died. She was nervous, and any sudden noise made her put her hands quickly to her throat. Her leg still hurt; she rubbed it often and patted it, as if to console it.

It took six months for the Red Cross Hospital, and even longer for Dr. Sasaki, to get back to normal. Until the city restored electric power, the hospital had to limp along with the aid of a Japanese Army generator in its backyard. Operating tables, X-ray machines, dentist chairs, everything complicated and essential came in a trickle of charity from other cities. In Japan, face is important even to institutions, and long before the Red Cross Hospital was back to par on basic medical equipment, its directors put up a new yellow brick veneer façade, so the hospital became the handsomest building in Hiroshima—from the street. For the first four months, Dr. Sasaki was the only surgeon on the staff and he almost never left the building; then, gradually, he began to take an interest in his own life again. He got married in March. He gained back some of the weight he lost, but his appetite remained only fair; before the bombing, he used to eat four rice balls at every meal, but a year after it he could manage only two. He felt tired all the time. "But I have to realize," he said, "that the whole community is tired."

A YEAR after the bomb was dropped, Miss Sasaki was a cripple; Mrs. Nakamura was destitute; Father Kleinsorge was back in the hospital; Dr. Sasaki was not capable of the work he once could do; Dr. Fujii had lost the thirty-room hospital it took him many years to acquire, and had no prospects of rebuilding it; Mr. Tanimoto's church had been ruined and he no longer had his exceptional vitality. The lives of these six people, who were among the luckiest in Hiroshima, would never be the same. What they thought of their experiences and of the use of the atomic bomb was, of course, not unanimous. One feeling they did seem to share, however, was a curious kind of elated community spirit, something like that of the Londoners after their blitz—a pride in the way they and their fellow-survivors had stood up to a dreadful ordeal. Just before the anniversary, Mr. Tanimoto wrote in a letter to an American some words which expressed this feeling: "What a heartbreaking scene this was the first night! About midnight I landed on the riverbank. So many injured people lied on the ground that I made my way by striding over them. Repeating 'Excuse me,' I forwarded and carried a tub of water with me and gave a cup of water to each one of them. They raised their upper bodies slowly and accepted a cup of water with a bow and drunk quietly and, spilling any remnant, gave back a cup with hearty expression of their thankfulness, and said, 'I couldn't help my sister, who was buried under the house, because I had to take care of my mother who got a deep wound on her eye and our house soon set fire and we hardly escaped. Look, I lost my home, my family, and at last my-self bitterly injured. But now I have gotted my mind to dedicate what I have and to complete the war for our country's sake.' Thus they pledged to me, even women and children did the same. Being entirely tired I lied down on the ground among them, but couldn't sleep at all. Next morning I found many men and women dead, whom I gave water last night. But, to my great surprise, I never heard any one cried in disorder, even though they suffered in great agony. They died in silence, with no grudge, setting their teeth to bear it. All for the country!

"Dr. Y. Hiraiwa, professor of Hiroshima University of Literature and Science, and one of my church members, was buried by the bomb under the two storied house with his son, a student of Tokyo University. Both of them could not move an inch under tremendously heavy pressure. And the house already caught fire. His son said, 'Father, we can do nothing except make our mind up to consecrate our lives for the country. Let us give *Banzai* to our Emperor.' Then the father followed after his son, *'Tenno-heika, Banzai, Banzai, Banzai!'* In the result, Dr. Hiraiwa said, 'Strange to say, I felt calm and bright and peaceful spirit in my heart, when I chanted *Banzai* to Tenno.' Afterward his son got out and digged down and pulled out his father and thus they were saved. In thinking of their experience of that time Dr. Hiraiwa repeated, 'What a fortunate that we are Japanese! It was my first time I ever tasted such a beautiful spirit when I decided to die for our Emperor.'

"Miss Kayoko Nobutoki, a student of girl's high school, Hiroshima Jazabuin, and a daughter of my church member, was taking rest with her friends beside the heavy fence of the Buddhist Temple. At the moment the atomic bomb was dropped, the fence fell upon them. They could not move a bit under such a heavy fence and then smoke entered into even a crack and choked their breath. One of the girls begun to sing *Kimi ga yo*, national anthem, and others followed in chorus and died. Meanwhile one of them found a crack and struggled hard to get out. When she was taken in the Red Cross Hospital she told how her friends died, tracing back in her memory to singing in chorus our national anthem. They were just 13 years old.

"Yes, people of Hiroshima died manly in the atomic bombing, believing that it was for Emperor's sake."

A surprising number of the people of Hiroshima remained more or less indifferent about the ethics of using the bomb. Possibly they were too terrified by it to want to think about it at all. Not many of them even bothered to find out much about what it was like. Mrs. Nakamura's conception of it—and awe of it—was typical. "The atom bomb," she would say when asked about it, "is the size of a matchbox. The heat of it is six thousand times that of the sun. It exploded in the air. There is some radium in it. I don't know just how it works, but when the radium is put together, it explodes." As for the use of the bomb, she would say, "It was war and we had to expect it." And then she would add, *"Shikata ga nai,"* a Japanese expression as common as, and corresponding to, the Russian word *"nichevo"*: "It can't be helped. Oh, well. Too bad." Dr. Fujii said approximately the same thing about the use of the bomb to Father Kleinsorge one evening, in German: *"Da ist nichts zu machen.* There's nothing to be done about it."

Many citizens of Hiroshima, however, continued to feel a hatred for Americans which nothing could possibly erase. "I see," Dr. Sasaki once said, "that they are holding a trial for war criminals in Tokyo just now. I think they ought to try the men who decided to use the bomb and they should hang them all."

Father Kleinsorge and the other German Jesuit priests, who, as foreigners, could be expected to take a relatively detached view, often discussed the ethics of using the bomb. One of them, Father Siemes, who was out at Nagatsuka at the time of the attack, wrote in a report to the Holy See in Rome: "Some of us consider the bomb in the same category as poison gas and were against its use on a civilian population. Others were of the opinion that in total war, as carried on in Japan, there was no difference between civilians and soldiers, and that the bomb itself was an effective force tending to end the bloodshed, warning Japan to surrender and thus to avoid total destruction. It seems logical that he who supports total war in principle cannot complain of a war against civilians. The crux

1 1 7

of the matter is whether total war in its present form is justifiable, even when it serves a just purpose. Does it not have material and spiritual evil as its consequences which far exceed whatever good might result? When will our moralists give us a clear answer to this question?"

It would be impossible to say what horrors were embedded in the minds of the children who lived through the day of the bombing in Hiroshima. On the surface, their recollections, months after the disaster, were of an exhilarating adventure. Toshio Nakamura, who was ten at the time of the bombing, was soon able to talk freely, even gaily, about the experience, and a few weeks before the anniversary he wrote the following matter-of-fact essay for his teacher at Nobori-cho Primary School: "The day before the bomb, I went for a swim. In the morning, I was eating peanuts. I saw a light. I was knocked to little sister's sleeping place. When we were saved, I could only see as far as the tram. My mother and I started to pack our things. The neighbors were walking around burned and bleeding. Hataya-*san* told me to run away with her. I said I wanted to wait for my mother. We went to the park. A whirlwind came. At night a gas tank burned and I saw the reflection in the river. We stayed in the park one night. Next day I went to Taiko Bridge and met my girl friends Kikuki and Murakami. They were looking for their mothers. But Kikuki's mother was wounded and Murakami's mother, alas was dead."

V · *The Aftermath*

1 · HATSUYO NAKAMURA

HATSUYO NAKAMURA, weak and destitute, began a courageous struggle, which would last for many years, to keep her children and herself alive.

She had her rusted Sankoku machine repaired and began to take in some sewing, and she did cleaning and laundry and washed dishes for neighbors who were somewhat better off than she was. But she got so tired that she had to take two days' rest for every three days she worked, and if she was obliged for some reason to work for a whole week, she had then to rest for three or four days. She earned barely enough for food.

At this precarious time she fell ill. Her belly began to swell up, and she had diarrhea and so much pain she could no longer work at all. A doctor, who lived nearby, came to see her and told her she had roundworm, and he said, incorrectly, "If it bites your intestine, you'll die." In those days, there was a shortage of chemical fertilizers in Japan, so farmers were using night soil, and as a consequence many people began to harbor parasites, which were not fatal in themselves but were seriously debilitating to those who had had radiation sickness. The doctor treated Nakamura-san (as he would have addressed her) with santonin, a somewhat dangerous medicine derived from certain varieties of artemisia. To pay the doctor, she was forced to sell her last valuable possession, her husband's sewing machine. She came to think of that act as marking the lowest and saddest moment of her whole life.

In referring to those who went through the Hiroshima and Nagasaki bombings, the Japanese tended to shy away from the term "survivors," because in its focus on being alive it might suggest some slight to the sacred dead. The class of people to which Nakamura-san belonged came, therefore, to be called by a more neutral name, "hibakusha"—literally, "explosion-affected persons." For more than a decade after the bombings, the hibakusha lived in an economic limbo, apparently because the Japanese government did not want to find itself saddled with anything like moral responsibility for heinous acts of the victorious United States. Although it soon became clear that many hibakusha suffered consequences of their exposure to the bombs which were quite different in nature and degree from those of survivors even of the

The Aftermath

ghastly fire bombings in Tokyo and elsewhere, the government made no special provision for their relief—until, ironically, after the storm of rage that swept across Japan when the twenty-three crewmen of a fishing vessel, the _Lucky Dragon No. 5_, and its cargo of tuna were irradiated by the American test of a hydrogen bomb at Bikini in 1954. It took three years even then for a relief law for the hibakusha to pass the Diet.

Though Nakamura-san could not know it, she thus had a bleak period ahead of her. In Hiroshima, the early postwar years were, besides, a time, especially painful for poor people like her, of disorder, hunger, greed, thievery, black markets. Non-hibakusha employers developed a prejudice against the survivors as word got around that they were prone to all sorts of ailments, and that even those, like Nakamura-san, who were not cruelly maimed and had not developed any serious overt symptoms were unreliable workers, since most of them seemed to suffer, as she did, from the mysterious but real malaise that came to be known as one kind of lasting A-bomb sickness: a nagging weakness and weariness, dizziness now and then, digestive troubles, all aggravated by a feeling of oppression, a sense of doom, for it was said that unspeakable diseases might at any time plant nasty flowers in the bodies of their victims, and even in those of their descendants.

As Nakamura-san struggled to get from day to day, she had no time for attitudinizing about the bomb or anything else. She was sustained, curiously, by a kind of passivity, summed up in a phrase she herself sometimes used—"*Shikata ga-nai,*" meaning, loosely, "It can't be helped." She was not religious, but she lived in a culture long colored by the Buddhist belief that resignation might lead to clear vision; she had shared with other citizens a deep feeling of powerlessness in the face of a state authority that had been divinely strong ever since the Meiji Restoration in 1868; and the hell she had witnessed and the terrible aftermath unfolding around her reached so far beyond human understanding that it was impossible to think of them as the work of resentable human beings, such as the pilot of the *Enola Gay,* or President Truman, or the scientists who had made the bomb—or even, nearer at hand, the Japanese militarists who had helped to bring on the war. The bombing almost seemed a natural disaster—one that it had simply been her bad luck, her fate (which must be accepted), to suffer.

When she had been wormed and felt slightly better, she made an arrangement to deliver bread for a baker named Takahashi, whose bakery was in Nobori-cho. On days when she had the strength to do it, she would take orders for bread from retail shops in her neighborhood, and the next morning she would pick up the requisite number of loaves and carry them in baskets and boxes through the streets to the stores. It was exhausting work, for which she earned the equivalent of about fifty cents a day. She had to take frequent rest days.

After some time, when she was feeling a bit stronger, she took up another kind of peddling. She would get up in the dark and trundle a borrowed two-wheeled push-cart for two hours across the city to a section called Eba, at the mouth of one of the seven estuarial rivers that branch from the Ota River through Hiroshima. There, at daylight, fishermen would cast their leaded skirtlike nets for sardines, and she would help them to gather up the catch when they hauled it in. Then she would push the cart back to Nobori-cho and sell the fish for them from door to door. She earned just enough for food.

A couple of years later, she found work that was better suited to her need for occasional rest, because within certain limits she could do it on her own time. This was a job of collecting money for deliveries of the Hiroshima paper, the *Chugoku Shimbun,* which most people in the city read. She had to cover a big territory, and often her clients were not at home or pleaded that they couldn't pay just then, so she would have to go back again and again. She earned the equivalent of about twenty dollars a month at this job. Every day, her willpower and her weariness seemed to fight to an uneasy draw.

IN 1951, after years of this drudgery, it was Nakamura-san's good luck, her fate (which must be accepted), to become eligible to move into a better house. Two years earlier, a Quaker professor of dendrology from the University of Washington named Floyd W. Schmoe, driven, apparently, by deep urges for expiation and reconciliation, had come to Hiroshima, assembled a team of carpenters, and, with his own hands and theirs, begun building a series of Japanese-style houses for victims of the bomb; in all, his team eventually built twenty-one. It was to one of these houses that Nakamura-san had the good fortune to be assigned. The Japanese measure their houses by multiples of the area of the floor-covering *tsubo* mat, a little less than four square yards, and the Dr. Shum-o houses, as the Hiroshimans called them, had two rooms of six mats each. This was a big step up for the Nakamuras. This home was redolent of new wood and clean matting. The rent, payable to the city government, was the equivalent of about a dollar a month.

Despite the family's poverty, the children seemed to be growing normally. Yaeko and Myeko, the two daughters, were anemic, but all three had so far escaped any of the more serious complications that so many young hibakusha were suffering. Yaeko, now fourteen, and Myeko, eleven, were in middle school. The boy, Toshio, ready to enter high school, was going to have to earn money to attend it, so he took up delivering papers to the places from which his mother was collecting. These were some distance from their Dr. Shum-o house, and they had to commute at odd hours by streetcar.

The old hut in Nobori-cho stood empty for a time, and, while continuing with her newspaper collections, Nakamura-san converted it into a small street shop for children, selling sweet potatoes, which she roasted, and *dagashi*, or little candies and rice cakes, and cheap toys, which she bought from a wholesaler.

All along, she had been collecting for papers from a small company, Suyama Chemical, that made mothballs sold under the trade name Paragen. A friend of hers worked there, and one day the friend suggested to Nakamura-san that she join the company, helping wrap the product in its packages. The owner, Nakamura-san learned, was a compassionate man, who did not share the bias of many employers against hibakusha; he had several on his staff of twenty women wrappers. Nakamura-san objected that she couldn't work more than a few days at a time; the friend persuaded her that Mr. Suyama would understand that.

So she began. Dressed in company uniforms, the women stood, somewhat bent over, on either side of a couple of conveyor belts, working as fast as possible to wrap two kinds of Paragen in cellophane. Paragen had a dizzying odor, and at first it made one's eyes smart. Its substance, powdered paradichlorobenzene, had been compressed into lozenge-shaped mothballs and into larger spheres, the size of small oranges, to be hung in Japanese-style toilets, where their rank pseudo-medicinal smell would offset the unpleasantness of non-flushing facilities.

Nakamura-san was paid, as a beginner, a hundred and seventy yen—then less than fifty cents—a day. At first, the work was confusing, terribly tiring, and a bit sickening. Her boss worried about her paleness. She had to take many days off. But little by little she became used to the factory. She made friends. There was a family atmosphere. She got raises. In the two ten-minute breaks, morning and afternoon, when the moving belt stopped, there was a birdsong of gossip and laughter, in which she joined. It appeared that all along there had been, deep in her temperament, a core of cheerfulness, which must have fuelled her long fight against A-bomb lassitude, something warmer and more vivifying than mere submission, than saying, *"Shikata ga-nai."* The other women took to her; she was constantly doing them small favors. They began calling her, affectionately, *Oba-san*—roughly, "Auntie."

She worked at Suyama for thirteen years. Though her energy still paid its dues, from time to time, to the A-bomb syndrome, the searing experiences of that day in 1945 seemed gradually to be receding from the front of her mind.

THE *Lucky Dragon No. 5* episode took place in 1954, the year after Nakamura-san started working for Suyama Chemical. In the ensuing fever of outrage in the country, the provision of adequate medical care for the victims of the Hiroshima and Nagasaki bombs finally became a political issue. Almost every year since 1946, on the anniversary of the Hiroshima bombing a Peace Memorial Meeting had been held in a park that the city planners had set aside, during the city's rebuilding, as a center of remembrance, and on August 6, 1955, delegates from all over the world gathered there for the first World Conference against Atomic and Hydrogen Bombs. On its second day, a number of hibakusha tearfully testified to the government's neglect of their plight. Japanese political parties took up the cause, and in 1957 the Diet at last passed the A-Bomb Victims Medical Care Law. This law and its subsequent modifications defined four classes of people who would be eligible for support: those who had been in the city limits on the day of the bombing; those who had entered an area within two kilometres of the hypocenter in the first fourteen days after it; those who had come into physical contact with bomb victims, in administering first aid or in disposing of their bodies; and those who had been embryos in the wombs of women in any of the first three categories. These hibakusha were entitled to receive so-called health books, which would entitle them to free medical treatment. Later revisions of the law provided for monthly allowances to victims suffering from various aftereffects.

Like a great many hibakusha, Nakamura-san had kept away from all the agitation, and, in fact, also like many other survivors, she did not even bother to get a health book for a couple of years after they were issued. She had been too poor to keep going to doctors, so she had got into the habit of coping alone, as best she could, with whatever ailed her. Besides, she shared with some other survivors a suspicion of ulterior motives on the part of the political-minded people who took part in the annual ceremonies and conferences.

Nakamura-san's son, Toshio, right after his graduation from high school, went to work for the bus division of the Japanese National Railways. He was in the administrative offices, working first on timetables, later in accounting. When he was in his mid-twenties, a marriage was arranged for him, through a relative who knew the bride's family. He built an addition to the Dr. Shum-o house, moved in, and began to contribute to his mother's support. He made her a present of a new sewing machine.

Yaeko, the older daughter, left Hiroshima when she

was fifteen, right after graduating from middle school, to help an ailing aunt who ran a *ryokan*, a Japanese-style inn. There, in due course, she fell in love with a man who ate at the inn's restaurant, and she made a love marriage.

After graduating from high school, Myeko, the most susceptible of the three children to the A-bomb syndrome, eventually became an expert typist and took up instructing at typing schools. In time, a marriage was arranged for her.

Like their mother, all three children avoided pro-hibakusha and antinuclear agitation.

IN 1966, Nakamura-san, having reached the age of fifty-five, retired from Suyama Chemical. At the end, she was being paid thirty thousand yen, or about eighty-five dollars, a month. Her children were no longer dependent on her, and Toshio was ready to take on a son's responsibility for his aging mother. She felt at home in her body now; she rested when she needed to, and she had no worries about the cost of medical care, for she had finally picked up Health Book No.1023993. It was time for her to enjoy life. For her pleasure in being able to give gifts, she took up embroidery and the dressing of traditional *kimekomi* dolls, which are supposed to bring good luck. Wearing a bright kimono, she went once a week to dance at the Study Group of Japanese Folk Music. In set movements, with expressive gestures, her hands now and then tucking up the long folds of the kimono sleeves, and with head held high, she danced,

moving as if floating, with thirty agreeable women to a
song of celebration of entrance into a house:

> May your family flourish
> For a thousand generations,
> For eight thousand generations.

About a year after Nakamura-san retired, she was invited by an organization called the Bereaved Families'
Association to take a train trip with about a hundred
other war widows to visit the Yasukuni Shrine, in Tokyo.
This holy place, established in 1869, was dedicated to
the spirits of all the Japanese who had died in wars
against foreign powers, and could be thought roughly
analogous, in terms of its symbolism for the nation, to
the Arlington National Cemetery—with the difference
that souls, not bodies, were hallowed there. The shrine
was considered by many Japanese to be a focus of a still
smoldering Japanese militarism, but Nakamura-san, who
had never seen her husband's ashes and had held on to
a belief that he would return to her someday, was ob-
livious of all that. She found the visit baffling. Besides
the Hiroshima hundred, there were huge crowds of
women from other cities on the shrine grounds. It was
impossible for her to summon up a sense of her dead
husband's presence, and she returned home in an uneasy state of mind.

JAPAN was booming. Things were still rather tight for
the Nakamuras, and Toshio had to work very long hours,

but the old days of bitter struggle began to seem remote. In 1975, one of the laws providing support to the hibakusha was revised, and Nakamura-san began to receive a so-called health-protection allowance of six thousand yen, then about twenty dollars, a month; this would gradually be increased to more than twice that amount. She also received a pension, toward which she had contributed at Suyama, of twenty thousand yen, or about sixty-five dollars, a month; and for several years she had been receiving a war widow's pension of another twenty thousand yen a month. With the economic upswing, prices had, of course, risen steeply (in a few years Tokyo would become the most expensive city in the world), but Toshio managed to buy a small Mitsubishi car, and occasionally he got up before dawn and rode a train for two hours to play golf with business associates. Yaeko's husband ran a shop for sales and service of air conditioners and heaters, and Myeko's husband ran a newsstand and candy shop near the railroad station.

In May each year, around the time of the Emperor's birthday, when the trees along broad Peace Boulevard were at their feathery best and banked azaleas were everywhere in bloom, Hiroshima celebrated a flower festival. Entertainment booths lined the boulevard, and there were long parades, with floats and bands and thousands of marchers. In the fortieth year after the bombing, Nakamura-san danced with the women of the folk-dance association, six dancers in each of sixty rows. They danced to *Oiwai-Ondo*, a song of happiness, lifting their arms in gestures of joy and clapping in rhythms of threes:

The Aftermath

Green pine trees, cranes and
    turtles . . .
You must tell a story of your hard
    times
And laugh twice.

The bombing had been four decades ago. How far away it seemed!

The sun blazed that day. The measured steps and the constant lifting of the arms for hours at a time were tiring. In midafternoon, Nakamura-san suddenly felt woozy. The next thing she knew, she was being lifted, to her great embarrassment and in spite of begging to be let alone, into an ambulance. At the hospital, she said she was fine; all she wanted was to go home. She was allowed to leave.

2 · DR. TERUFUMI SASAKI

DR. TERUFUMI SASAKI was still racked by memories of the appalling days and nights right after the explosion—memories it would be his lifework to distance himself from. Besides his duties as a junior surgeon at the Red Cross Hospital, he now had to spend every Thursday across the city at the University of Hiroshima, to chip away at his doctoral dissertation on appendicial tuberculosis. As was the custom in Japan, he had been permitted to start his practice as soon as he was graduated from medical school. It took most young internes five years of additional study to get their actual doctoral degree; in Dr. Sasaki's case, it was, for various reasons, to take ten.

He had been commuting during that year from the small town of Mukaihara, where his mother lived, about an hour by train from the city. His family had money— and, indeed, over the years it turned out (as it did for a great many Japanese doctors) that the most efficacious medicine for whatever ailed him would be cash or credit, the larger the dosage the better. His grandfather had been a landlord and had accumulated wide mountain tracts of valuable woodland. His late father, a doctor, had earned good money in a private clinic. During the turbulent time of hunger and crime after the bombing, thieves had broken into two fortlike storage repositories next to his mother's house and taken many valued heirlooms, including a lacquer box given to the doctor's grandfather by the Emperor, an ancient case for writing brushes and ink blocks, and a classic painting of a tiger, alone worth ten million yen, or more than twenty-five thousand dollars.

His marriage was working out well. He had been able to pick and choose. There had not been many such eligible young men as he in Mukaihara, and numerous marriage brokers had sounded him out. He had followed up some of these feelers. One father of an offered bride had received his agent and turned him down. Perhaps this was because Dr. Sasaki had a reputation of having been a very bad boy, a "tomcat," some said, when he was young; and the father may have known about his illegal treatment of patients in Mukaihara in the evenings after his work at the Red Cross Hospital. But perhaps it was also because the father was overcautious. It was said of him that he not only followed the Japanese saying, "Check an old iron bridge well before crossing," he would not cross even after checking. Dr. Sasaki, never in his life having experienced such a rebuff, had decided that this was the girl for him, and with the help of two persistent go-betweens he had eventually won the wary parent over. Now, married only a few months, he was quickly learning that his wife was wiser and more sensible than he.

Much of Dr. Sasaki's work as a surgeon at the Red Cross Hospital in the next five years was in the removal of keloid scars—hideously ugly, thick, itchy, rubbery, copper-red crablike growths that often formed over bad burns that hibakusha had suffered, and particularly those victims who had been exposed to the great heat of the bomb within two kilometres of the hypocenter. In dealing with the keloids, Dr. Sasaki and his colleagues were groping in the dark, because they had no reliable literature to guide them. They found that after the bulbous scars had been removed they often recurred. Some, if they were left unattended, became infected, and others caused underlying muscles to tense up. He and his colleagues eventually came to the reluctant conclusion that they should not have operated on many of the keloids.

The scars tended in time to shrink spontaneously, and could then be more easily excised, or be left alone.

In 1951, Dr. Sasaki decided to quit working for the hospital, with its awful memories, and to set himself up, as his father had done, in a private clinic in Mukaihara. He was ambitious. He had had an older brother, who, according to the custom of Japanese medical families, had been expected to succeed to the father's practice; the second son would have to make his own way, and in 1939, urged by the propaganda of the time to seek a fortune in the vast undeveloped reaches of China, Teru-fumi Sasaki had gone there and had studied at the Japanese Eastern Medical University, in Tsingtao. He had graduated and returned to Hiroshima shortly before the bombing. His brother had been killed in the war, so the way was clear for him—not only to start a practice in his father's town but also to withdraw from Hiroshima and, in effect, from being a hibakusha. For the next four decades, he also never spoke to anyone about the hours and days after the bombing.

His grandfather having deposited large sums in the Bank of Hiroshima, Dr. Sasaki went to it confidently expecting a big loan to help him get started. But the bank said that a clinic in such a small town could easily fail, and it put a cap on his credit of three hundred thousand yen, then less than a thousand dollars. So Dr. Sasaki started treating patients in his wife's parents' house. He performed simple surgery—on appendixes, gastric ulcers, compound fractures—but he also rather daringly practiced every other sort of medicine, too, except gyne-cology and obstetrics. He did surprisingly well. Before long, he was getting nearly a hundred patients a day. Some came to him from considerable distances. The bank noticed, and his limit of credit rose to a million yen.

In 1954, he put up a proper clinic building within the compound of his wife's family; it was a two-story struc-ture with nineteen beds for in-patients and a total floor space of two hundred and eighty mats. He financed the building with a loan of three hundred thousand yen from the bank and by selling timber from the lands he had inherited from his grandfather. In the new clinic, with a staff of five nurses and three on-the-job trainees, and working himself without pause six days a week from eight-thirty in the morning till six in the evening, he continued to prosper.

LONG before this, doctors in Hiroshima had begun to find that there were much more serious consequences of exposure to the bomb than the traumatic wounds and keloid scars that had been so dramatically visible in the early days. The violent symptoms of primary radiation sickness wore off in time in most patients, but it soon became clear that hibakusha were liable to deeper and far more dangerous sequels from the enormous doses of radiation dealt them by the bomb. Above all, it was evident by 1950 that the incidence of leukemia in hi-bakusha was much higher than normal; among those who had been exposed within one kilometre of the hy-pocenter, the incidence was reported to be between ten and fifty times above the norm. Over the years, the appearance of "purple spots," tiny surface hemorrhages symptomatic of leukemia, came to be dreaded by hibakusha. And, later on, other forms of cancer besides leukemia, with longer periods of latency, were showing up at higher than normal rates: carcinomas of the thyroid, the lungs, the breast, the salivary glands, the stomach, the liver, the urinary tract, and the male and female reproductive organs. Some survivors—even children—were developing what were called A-bomb cataracts. Some exposed children were growing up stunted, and one of the most shocking findings was that some children who had been in their mothers' womb at the time of the bombing were born with heads smaller than normal. Because it was known that radiation affected the genes of laboratory animals, a fear spread among many hibakusha that future descendants of the survivors might be subject to mutations. (It was the late sixties before analyses indeed showed some chromosome aberrations in Hiroshima and Nagasaki survivors, and it would, of course, take much longer to tell what, if any, effects there would be on their progeny.) There were several ailments, less life-threatening than the cancers, that were thought by many doctors—and by most of the people who were subject to them—to have resulted from exposure to the bomb: several sorts of anemia, liver dysfunction, sexual problems, endocrine disorders, accelerated aging, and the not-quite-really-sick yet undeniable debilitation of which so many complained.

Dr. Sasaki, who had himself suffered nothing but this

last, paid little or no attention to any of these revelations. He did not follow them closely in the medical journals. In his town in the hills, he treated few hibakusha. He lived enclosed in the present tense.

IN 1963, wanting to get caught up on the latest developments in anaesthesia, Dr. Sasaki went to the Yokohama Red Cross Hospital to learn about them from its director general, Dr. Tatsutaro Hattori. As chief of surgery at the Hiroshima hospital, Dr. Hattori had been Dr. Sasaki's boss there; he had come down with radiation sickness after the bombing and had moved to Yokohama. Dr. Hattori suggested that Dr. Sasaki might as well have a thorough physical examination, taking advantage of the hospital's up-to-the-minute equipment, while he was there, and Dr. Sasaki agreed. A tomographic scan of his chest showed up a shadow in the left lung. Dr. Sasaki smoked. Without going into what had been learned about the incidence of lung cancer in hibakusha, perhaps supposing that Dr. Sasaki would know all about such things, Dr. Hattori recommended a biopsy. It was done, and when Dr. Sasaki came out of the anaesthetic he found that his entire left lung had been removed.

A few hours after the operation, a ligature of one of the blood vessels into the lung cavity gave way, and Dr. Sasaki suffered severe hemorrhaging for nearly a week. One day toward the end of that time, as he continued to cough up blood and grew worrisomely feeble, there gathered around him what he construed as a death-watch: his wife, Dr. Hattori, the hospital matron, several nurses. He thanked them, said goodbye to his wife, and died.

Or, rather, he thought he died. Some time later, he regained consciousness and found himself on the mend.

In later years, Dr. Sasaki came to think of that experience as the most important of his life—more important than the bombing. Haunted by the loneliness he had felt when he thought he was dying, he now did his best to move closer to his wife and his children—two sons and two daughters. An aunt startled him one day by saying, "You are lucky, Terufumi. After all, *i wa jinjutsu*—medicine is the art of compassion." He had never thought about the meaning of this saying, which is held up before all young Japanese training to be doctors. He determined thenceforth to be calm and composed, and not to leave undone anything he could do for a patient. He would try to be kind to people he detested. He would give up hunting and mah-jongg. His wife said, "You've reached maturity in your forties. I grew up when I was in my twenties."

He did not give up cigarettes.

In 1972, Dr. Sasaki's wife died of breast cancer—the third crisis of his life. He achieved now another sort of loneliness connected with death, this one nontransient and intense. He threw himself more tirelessly than ever into his work.

His wife's death and his own near-death, together with

his realization that he was no longer young, started him thinking about the elderly, and he decided to build a much larger new clinic, where he would practice geriatric medicine. This branch of the compassionate art was attracting some of the ablest Japanese doctors, and it also happened to be growing extremely lucrative. As he put it to friends, who laughed at what they considered his overreaching, everyone after sixty had aches and pains, everyone as old as that needed massage, heat therapy, acupuncture, moxa, and comfort from a friendly physician—they would come in flocks.

By 1977, Dr. Sasaki's credit with the Bank of Hiroshima had soared, and it granted him a loan of nineteen million yen, or about eighty thousand dollars. With this money he put up, on land on the edge of town, an imposing four-story concrete building, with nineteen beds for in-patients and with extensive facilities for rehabilitation, and also with a splendid apartment for himself. He took on a staff of three acupuncturists, three therapists, eight nurses, and fifteen paramedics and maintenance people. His two sons, Yoshihisa and Ryuji, by now both doctors, came to help out in specially busy periods.

He was right about the flocks. Again he worked from eight-thirty to six, six days a week, and he saw an average of two hundred and fifty patients a day. Some came to him from cities as far away as Kure, Ondo, and Akitsu, on the coast, and others from villages all over the prefecture. Taking advantage of huge tax deductions that Japanese doctors could claim, he saved large sums, and as he returned money on his bank loans the bank kept raising his line of credit. He got the idea of building an old-people's home, which would cost two hundred million yen. It would be necessary to get approval for this project from the Takata County Medical Association. He submitted plans. He was turned down. Soon afterward, a leading member of the association built in the city of Yoshida just such a home as Dr. Sasaki had proposed.

Undaunted, Dr. Sasaki, aware that the three foremost pleasures of his elderly patients were family visits, good food, and a relaxed bath time, used the bank's loans to build, on the site of his former clinic, a luxurious bathhouse. This was ostensibly for patients, but he opened it to the townspeople as well, charging more for admission than the usual public bathhouse did; its tubs, after all, were of marble. He spent half a million (deductible) yen a month on its upkeep.

Every morning, Dr. Sasaki met with the entire staff of the clinic. He had a favorite lecture: Do not work primarily for money; do your duty to patients first and let the money follow; our life is short, we don't live twice; the whirlwind will pick up the leaves and spin them, but then it will drop them and they will form a pile.

Dr. Sasaki's own pile grew and grew. His life was insured for a hundred million yen; he was insured against malpractice for three hundred million yen. He drove a white BMW. Rare vases stood on chests in his living room. In spite of the enormous tax deductions allowed Japanese doctors, he had come to be the payer of the highest income tax in Takata County (population thirty-seven thousand), and his tax was among the ten highest in all of Hiroshima Prefecture (twelve cities and sixty-eight towns in fifteen counties; population two million seven hundred thousand).

He had a new idea. He would drill down next to the clinic for subterranean hot water, to fill hot-springs baths. He hired the Tokyo Geological Engineering Company to do a survey, and it assured him that if he drilled down eight hundred metres he would get from sixty to a hundred litres of water a minute, at between 79 and 86 degrees Fahrenheit. He had visions of a hot-springs spa; he calculated that he could supply water for hot baths in three hotels. He started digging in June 1985.

Dr. sasaki began to be considered a bit strange by Hiroshima doctors. He was not attracted, as they were, to the exclusive high society of the medical associations. Instead, he went in for such things as sponsoring a Mukaihara contest in gateball, a primitive variant of croquet; he often wore a necktie—which cost him five thousand yen, or twenty dollars—with *Gate Ball* embroidered across it in English script. His principal pleasure, apart from his work, was to take an occasional trip to Hiroshima to eat Chinese food in the basement of the Grand Hotel, lighting up, at the end of the meal, a cigarette of the brand Mild Seven, which had printed on its packet, besides its name in English, this courteous Japanese admonition: "Let's be careful not to smoke too much, for the sake of our health."

He could face Hiroshima now, because a gaudy phoenix had risen from the ruinous desert of 1945: a remarkably beautiful city of more than a million inhabitants—only one in ten of whom was a hibakusha—with tall modern buildings on broad, tree-lined avenues crowded with Japanese cars, all of which had English lettering on them and appeared to be brand-new; a city of strivers and sybarites, with seven hundred and fifty-three bookstores and two thousand three hundred and fifty-six bars. If past memories did stir up in him, Dr. Sasaki had come to be able to live with his one bitter regret: that in the shambles of the Red Cross Hospital in those first days after the bombing it had not been possible, beyond a certain point, to keep track of the identities of those whose corpses were dragged out to the mass cremations, with the result that nameless souls might still, all these years later, be hovering there, unattended and dissatisfied.

3 · FATHER WILHELM KLEINSORGE

BACK IN THE HOSPITAL in Tokyo for the second time, Father Kleinsorge was suffering from fever, diarrhea, wounds that would not heal, wildly fluctuating blood counts, and utter exhaustion. For the rest of his life, his was to be a classic case history of that vague, borderline form of A-bomb sickness in which a person's body developed a rich repertory of symptoms, few of which could be positively attributed to radiation, but many of which turned up in hibakusha, in various combinations and degrees, so often as to be blamed by some doctors and almost all patients on the bomb.

Father Kleinsorge lived this life of misery with the most extraordinarily selfless spirit. After his discharge from the hospital, he returned to the tiny Noborimachi chapel he had helped build, and there he continued his self-abnegating pastoral life.

In 1948, he was named priest of the much grander Misasa church, in another part of town. There were not yet many tall buildings in the city, and neighbors called the big church the Misasa Palace. A convent of Helpers of Holy Souls was attached to the church, and besides his priestly duties of conducting Mass, hearing confessions, and teaching Bible classes he ran eight-day retreats for novices and Sisters of the convent, during which the women, given Communion and instructed by him from day to day, would maintain silence. He still visited Sasaki-san and other hibakusha who were sick and wounded, and he would even babysit for young mothers. He often went to the sanatorium at Saijyo, an hour by train from the city, to comfort tubercular patients.

Father Kleinsorge was briefly hospitalized in Tokyo twice more. His German Jesuit colleagues were of the opinion that in all his work he was a little too much concerned for others, and not enough for himself. Beyond his own stubborn sense of mission, he had taken on himself the Japanese spirit of *enryo*—setting the self apart, putting the wishes of others first. They thought he might literally kill himself with kindness to others; he was too *rücksichtsvoll*, they said—too regardful. When gifts of delicacies came from relatives in Germany, he gave them all away. When he got penicillin from an Occupation doctor, he gave it to parishioners who were not as sick as he. (Among his many other complaints, he had syphilis, which he had apparently caught from transfusions in one of his hospital stays; it was cured eventually.) He gave lessons on the catechism when he had a high fever. After he came back from a long hike of pastoral calls, the Misasa housekeeper would see him collapse on the steps of his rectory, head down—a figure, it seemed, of utter defeat. The next day, he would be out in the streets again.

Gradually, over years of this unremitting labor, he gathered his modest harvest: some four hundred baptisms, some forty marriages.

FATHER KLEINSORGE loved the Japanese and their ways. One of his German colleagues, Father Berzikofer, jokingly said that Father Kleinsorge was married to Japan. Shortly after he moved to the Misasa church, he read that a new law on naturalization had been passed by the Diet, with these requirements: that one live in Japan for at least five years, be over twenty years old and mentally sound, be of good character, be able to support oneself, and be able to accept single nationality. He hastened to submit proofs that he met all these, and after some months of review he was accepted. He registered himself as a Japanese citizen under the name he would henceforth bear: Father Makoto Takakura.

For a few months in the spring and summer of 1956, his poor health declining still further, Father Takakura filled a temporary vacancy in a small parish in the Noborimachi district. Five years before that, the Reverend Mr. Kiyoshi Tanimoto, whom Father Takakura knew well, had begun giving Bible classes to a group of girls whose faces had been disfigured by keloids. Later, some of them had been taken, as so-called Hiroshima Maidens, to the United States for plastic surgery. One of them, Tomoko Nakabayashi, whom Father Takakura had converted and baptized, died on an operating table at Mount Sinai Hospital in New York. Her ashes were carried to her family when the first group of Maidens returned to Hiroshima that summer of 1956, and it fell to Father Takakura to preside at her funeral. During it, he nearly fainted.

At Noborimachi, he began instructing the female members, a mother and two daughters, of a wealthy and cultured family named Naganishi. Feverish or not, he went to them, always on foot, every evening. Sometimes he would arrive early; he would pace up and down the street outside, then ring the bell at precisely seven o'clock. He would look at himself in a hall mirror, adjust his hair and habit, and enter the living room. He would teach for an hour; then the Naganishis would serve tea and sweets, and he and they would chat until exactly ten. He felt at home in that house. The younger daughter, Hisako, became devoted to him, and when, after eighteen months, his various symptoms grew so bad that he was going to have to be hospitalized she asked him to baptize her, and he did, on the day before he entered the Hiroshima Red Cross Hospital for an entire year's stay.

His most disturbing complaint was a weird infection in his fingers, which had become bloated with pus and would not heal. He had fever and flulike symptoms. His white blood count was seriously low, and he had pain in his knees, particularly the left one, and in other joints. His fingers were operated on and slowly healed. He was treated for leukopenia. Before his discharge, an ophthalmologist found that he had the beginnings of an A-bomb cataract.

He returned to the large Misasa congregation, but it was harder and harder for him to carry the kind of overload he cherished. He developed back pain, which was caused, doctors said, by a kidney stone; he passed it. Dragged down by constant pain and by infections that were abetted by his shortage of white cells, he limped through his days, pushing himself beyond his strength.

Finally, in 1961, he was mercifully put out to pasture by the diocese, in a tiny church in the country town of Mukaihara—the town where Dr. Sasaki was flourishing in his private clinic.

The Aftermath

THE compound of the Mukaihara church, at the crest
of a steep rise from the town, enclosed a small chapel,
with an oaken table for an altar and with space for a
flock of about twenty to kneel, Japanese-fashion, on a
spread of tatami matting; and, uphill, a cramped parsonage. Father Takakura chose as his bedroom in the
parsonage a room no more than six feet square and as
bare as a monk's cell; he ate in another such cell, next
to it; and the kitchen and bathroom, beyond, were dark,
chilly, sunken rooms, no larger than the others. Across
a narrow corridor running the length of the building
were an office and a much larger bedroom, which Father
Takakura, true to his nature, reserved for guests.

When he first arrived, he felt enterprising, and, on
the principle that souls are best caught while unripe, he
had builders add two rooms to the chapel and started
in them what he called the St. Mary's Kindergarten. So
began a bleak life for four Catholics: the priest, two
Japanese sisters to teach the babies, and a Japanese woman
to cook. Few believers came to church. His parish consisted of four previously converted families, about ten
worshippers in all. Some Sundays, no one showed up
for Mass.

After its first spurt, Father Takakura's energy rapidly
flagged. Once each week, he took a train to Hiroshima
and went to the Red Cross Hospital for a checkup. At
Hiroshima station, he picked up what he loved best to
read as he travelled—timetables with schedules of trains
going all over Honshu Island. The doctors injected ster-

oids in his painful joints and treated him for the chronic flulike symptoms, and once he reported he had found traces of blood in his underwear, which the doctors guessed came from new kidney stones.

In the village of Mukaihara, he tried to be as inconspicuous—as Japanese—as he could. He sometimes wore Japanese clothes. Not wanting to seem high-living, he never bought meat in the local market, but sometimes he smuggled some out from the city. A Japanese priest who occasionally came to see him, Father Hasegawa, admired his efforts to carry his naturalization through to perfection but found him in many ways unshakably German. He had a tendency when he was rebuffed in an undertaking to stubbornly push all the harder straight for it, whereas a Japanese would more tactfully look for some way around. Father Hasegawa noticed that when Father Takakura was hospitalized, he rigidly respected the hospital's visiting hours, and if people came, even from far away, to see him, outside proper hours, he refused to receive them. Once, eating with his friend, Father Hasegawa declined his host's offer of a bowl of rice; he said he was full. But then delicious pickles appeared, which caused a Japanese palate to cry out for rice, and he decided to have a bowl after all. Father Takakura was outraged (i.e., in his guest's view, German): How could he eat rice plus pickle when he had been too full to eat rice alone?

DURING this period, Father Takakura was one of many people whom Dr. Robert J. Lifton interviewed in preparing to write his book *Death in Life: Survivors of Hiroshima*. In one conversation the priest hinted that he realized he had achieved a truer identity as a hibakusha than as a Japanese:

> If a person says to me that he is weary [*darui*], if it is a hibakusha who says it, it gives me a different feeling than if he is an ordinary person. He doesn't have to explain. . . . He knows all of the uneasiness—all of the temptation to lose spirit and be depressed—and of then starting again to see if he can do his job. . . . If a Japanese hears the words "*tenno heika*" [His Majesty the Emperor], it is different from a Westerner hearing them—a very different feeling in the foreigner's heart from what is felt in the Japanese person's heart. It is a similar question in the case of one who is a victim and one who is not, when they hear about another victim. . . . I met a man one time . . . [who] said, "I experienced the atomic bomb"—and from then on the conversation changed. We both understood each other's feelings. Nothing had to be said.

In 1966, Father Takakura had to change cooks. A woman named Satsue Yoshiki, who was thirty-five years old, recently cured of tuberculosis, and recently baptized, had been told to report for an interview at the Mukaihara church. Having been given the Japanese name of the priest, she was astonished to be greeted by a big *gaijin*, a foreigner, dressed in a quilted Japanese gown. His face, which was rounded out and puffy (doubtless from medication), struck her as that of a baby. At once, indeed, there commenced a relationship, soon to blossom into one of complete mutual trust, in which her role seemed to be ambiguous: part daughter, part mother. His growing helplessness kept her in subjugation; she tenderly nursed him. Her cooking was primitive, his temper cranky. He had said he would eat anything, even Japanese noodles, but he was sharp with her about his food, as he had never been with anyone else. Once, he spoke of "strained baked potatoes" his real mother had cooked. She tried to make them. He said, "These are not like my mother's." He loved fried prawns and ate them when he went to Hiroshima for checkups. She tried to cook them He said, "These are burned." She stood beside him in the tiny eating room, her hands behind her gripping the doorjamb so tightly that in time its paint was all worn away. Yet he praised her, confided in her, joked with her, apologized to her each time he lost his temper. She thought him—under the shortness, which she attributed to pain—gentle, pure, patient, sweet, humorous, and deeply kind.

Once, on a late-spring day, not long after Yoshiki-san arrived, sparrows alighted in a persimmon tree outside his office window. He clapped his hands to drive them away, and soon there appeared on his palms purple spots of the sort that all hibakusha dreaded. The doctors in Hiroshima shook their heads. Who could say what they were? They seemed to be blood bruises, but his blood tests did not suggest leukemia. He had slight hemorrhages in his urinary tract. "What if I get blood in my brains?" he asked once. His joints still hurt. He developed liver dysfunction, high blood pressure, back pains, chest pains. An electrocardiogram turned up an anomaly. He was put on a drug to ward off a coronary attack, and on an antihypertensive drug. He was given steroids, hormones, an antidiabetic drug. "I don't take medicines, I eat them," he said to Yoshiki-san. In 1971, he was hospitalized for an operation to see whether his liver was cancerous; it was not.

All through this time of decline, a stream of visitors came to see him, thanking him for all he had done for them in the past. Hisako Naganishi, the woman he had baptized the day before his long hospitalization, was especially faithful; she brought him open-faced sandwiches on German rye bread, which he loved, and when Yoshiki-san needed a vacation, she would move in and tend him in her absence. Father Berzikofer would come for a few days at a time, and they would talk and drink a great deal of gin, which Father Takakura had also come to love.

ONE winter day at the beginning of 1976, Father Takakura slipped and fell on the steep icy path down to town. The next morning, Yoshiki-san heard him shouting her name. She found him in the bathroom, leaning over the washstand, unable to move. With all the strength of her love, she carried him—he weighed a hundred and seventy-five pounds—to his bed, and laid him down. For a month, he was unable to move. She improvised a bedpan, and cared for him day and night. Finally, she borrowed a wheelchair from the town office and took him to Dr. Sasaki's clinic. The two men had known each other years before, but now, one living in his monk's cell and the other in his grand apartment in the four-story clinic, they were light-years apart. Dr. Sasaki took an X-ray, saw nothing, diagnosed neuralgia, and advised massage. Father Takakura could not abide the idea of the usual female massager; a man was hired. During the workout, Father Takakura held Yoshiki-san's hand, and his face reddened. The pain was unbearable. Yoshiki-san hired a car and drove Father Takakura to the city, to the Red Cross Hospital. An X-ray on a bigger machine showed fractures of the eleventh and twelfth thoracic vertebrae. He was operated on to relieve pressure on the right sciatic nerve, and he was fitted with a corset.

From then on, he was bedridden. Yoshiki-san fed him, changed diapers that she made for him, and cleaned his body. He read the Bible and timetables—the only two sorts of texts, he told Yoshiki-san, that never told lies. He could tell you what train to take where, the price of food in the dining car, and how to change trains at such-and-such a station to save three hundred yen. One day, he called Yoshiki-san, greatly excited. He had found an error. Only the Bible told the truth!

His fellow-priests finally persuaded him to go to St. Luke's Hospital in Kobe. Yoshiki-san visited him, and he drew out from a book a copy of his chart, on which was written "A living corpse." He said he wanted to go home with her, and she took him. "Because of you, my soul has been able to get through purgatory," he said to her when he was in his own bed.

He weakened, and his fellow-priests moved him to a two-room house in a hollow just below their Novitiate, in Nagatsuka. Yoshiki-san told him she wanted to sleep in his room with him. No, he said, his vows would not permit that. She lied, saying that the father superior had ordered it. Greatly relieved, he allowed it. After that, he seldom opened his eyes. She fed him only ice cream. When visitors came, all he could say was "Thank you." He fell into a coma, and on November 19, 1977, with a doctor, a priest, and Yoshiki-san at his side, this explosion-affected person took a deep breath and died.

He was buried in a serene pine grove at the top of the hill above the Novitiate.

FATHER WILHELM M. TAKAKURA, S.J.
R.I.P.

The fathers and brothers of the Nagatsuka Novitiate noticed over the years that there were almost always fresh flowers at that grave.

4 · TOSHIKO SASAKI

IN AUGUST 1946, Toshiko Sasaki was slowly pulling out of the ordeal of pain and low spirits she had undergone during the year since the bombing. Her younger brother, Yasuo, and sister, Yaeko, had escaped injury on the day of the explosion because they had been in the family home in the suburb of Koi. Now, living with them there, she was just beginning to feel alive again, when a new blow came.

Three years earlier her parents had entered into marriage negotiations with another family, and she had met the proposed young man. The couple liked each other and decided to accept the arrangement. They rented a house to live in, but Toshiko's fiancé was suddenly drafted to China. She had heard he was back, but for a long time he had not come to see her. When he finally showed up, it seemed clear to both parties that the engagement was doomed. Each time the fiancé appeared, young Yasuo, for whom Toshiko felt responsible, would rush angrily out of the house. There were indications that the fiancé's family had had second thoughts about permitting their son to marry a hibakusha and a cripple. He stopped coming. He wrote letters full of symbolic, abstract images—especially butterflies—evidently trying to express his trembling uncertainty and, probably, guilt.

The only person who gave Toshiko any real comfort was Father Kleinsorge, who continued calling on her in Koi. He was clearly bent on converting her. The confident logic of his instruction did little to convince her, for she could not accept the idea that a God who had snatched away her parents and put her through such hideous trials was loving and merciful. She was, however, warmed and healed by the priest's faithfulness to her, for it was obvious that he, too, was weak and in pain, yet he walked great distances to see her.

Her house stood by a cliff, on which there was a grove of bamboo. One morning, she stepped out of the house, and the sun's rays glistening on the minnowlike leaves of the bamboo trees took her breath away. She felt an astonishing burst of joy—the first she had experienced in as long as she could remember. She heard herself reciting the Lord's Prayer.

In September, she was baptized. Father Kleinsorge was in the hospital in Tokyo, so Father Cieslik officiated.

Sasaki-san had some modest savings her parents had left, and she took in sewing to help support Yasuo and Yaeko, but she worried about the future. She taught herself to hobble without crutches. One day in the summer of 1947, she took the two for a swim at a beach at nearby Suginoura. There she got to talking with a young man, a Korean Catholic novice who was tending a group of Sunday-school children. After a while, he told her that he did not see how she could possibly go on as she was living, responsible for her brother and sister and so fragile herself. He told her of a good orphanage in Hiroshima called the Garden of Light. She entered the children in the orphanage, and a short time later she applied for a job as an attendant there. She was hired, and after that she had the solace of being with Yasuo and Yaeko.

She was good at her work. She seemed to have found

a calling, and the next year, convinced that her brother and sister were well cared for, she accepted a transfer to another orphanage, called the White Chrysanthemum Dormitory, in a suburb of Beppu, on the island of Kyushu, where it would be possible for her to receive professional child-care training. In the spring of 1949, she began commuting by train, about a half hour each way, to the city of Oita, to take courses at Oita University, and in September she passed an examination that qualified her as a nursery-school teacher. She worked at the White Chrysanthemum for six years.

Her lower left leg was badly bent, its knee was frozen, and its thigh was atrophied by the deep incisions Dr. Sasaki had made. The Sisters in charge of the orphanage arranged for her to enter the National Hospital in Beppu for orthopedic surgery. She was a patient there for fourteen months, during which she underwent three major operations: the first, not very successful, to help restore her thigh; the second to free her knee; and the third to rebreak her tibia and fibula and set them in something like their original alignment. After the hospitalization, she went to a nearby hot-springs therapeutic center for rehabilitation. Her leg would give her pain for the rest of her life, and her knee would never again bend all the way, but her legs were now more or less equal in length, and she could walk almost normally. She went back to work.

The White Chrysanthemum, with space for forty orphans, stood near an American Army base; on one side was an exercise field for the soldiers, and on the other were officers' houses. After the Korean War began, the base and the orphanage were packed. From time to time, a woman would bring in an infant whose father was an American soldier, never saying that she was the mother— usually that a friend had asked her to entrust the baby to the orphanage. Often, at night, nervous young soldiers, some white, some black, having sneaked off the base without leave, would come begging to see their offspring. They wanted to stare at the babies' faces. Some of them tracked down the mothers and married them, though they might never again see the children.

Sasaki-san felt compassion both for the mothers, some of whom were prostitutes, and for the fathers. She perceived the latter as confused boys of nineteen and twenty who as draftees were involved in a war they did not consider theirs, and who felt a rudimentary responsibility—or, at the very least, guilt—as fathers. These thoughts led her to an opinion that was unconventional for a hibakusha: that too much attention was paid to the power of the A-bomb, and not enough to the evil of war. Her rather bitter opinion was that it was the more lightly affected hibakusha and power-hungry politicians who focussed on the A-bomb, and that not enough thought was given to the fact that warfare had indiscriminately made victims of Japanese who had suffered atomic and incendiary bombings, Chinese civilians who had been attacked by the Japanese, reluctant young Japanese and American soldiers who were drafted to be killed or maimed, and, yes, Japanese prostitutes and their mixed-blood babies. She had firsthand knowledge of the cruelty of the atomic bomb, but she felt that more notice should be given to the causes than to the instruments of total war.

About once a year during this time, Sasaki-san travelled from Kyushu to Hiroshima to see her brother and sister, and, always, to call on Father Kleinsorge, now Takakura, at the Misasa church. On one trip, she saw her former fiancé on the street, and she was quite sure he saw her, but they did not speak. Father Takakura asked her, "Is your whole life going to be like this, working so hard? Shouldn't you be married? Or, if you choose not to marry, shouldn't you become a nun?" She thought long about his questions.

One day, at the White Chrysanthemum, she got an urgent message that her brother had been in an automobile accident and might die. She hurried to Hiroshima. Yasuo's car had been hit by a police patrol car; it had been the policeman's fault. Yasuo survived, but four ribs and both legs had been broken, his nose had been caved in, there was a permanent dent in his forehead, and he had lost the sight of one eye. Sasaki-san thought she was going to have to tend him and support him for good. She began taking accounting courses, and, after a few weeks, qualified as a Third Class Bookkeeper. But Yasuo made a remarkable recovery, and, using the compensation he was paid for the accident, he entered

a music school, to study composition. Sasaki-san went
back to the orphanage.

In 1954, Sasaki-san visited Father Takakura and said
that she knew now that she would never marry, and she
thought the time had come for her to go into a convent.
What convent would he recommend? He suggested the
French order of Auxiliatrices du Purgatoire, Helpers of
Holy Souls, whose convent was right there in Misasa.
Sasaki-san said she did not want to enter a society that
would make her speak foreign languages. He promised
her she could stay with Japanese.

She entered the convent, and in the very first days she
found that Father Takakura had lied to her. She was
going to have to learn Latin and French. She was told
that when the knock of reveille came in the morning,
she must cry out, *"Mon Jésus, miséricorde!"* The first night,
she wrote the words in ink on the palm of one hand, so
she could read them when she heard the knock the next
morning, but it turned out to be too dark.

She became afraid she might fail. She had no trouble
learning about Eugenie Smet, known as Blessed Mary
of Providence, the founder of the order, who in 1856
had started programs in Paris for care of the poor and
for home nursing and had eventually sent to China twelve
Sisters she had trained. But, at thirty, Sasaki-san felt too
old to be a schoolgirl learning Latin. She was confined
to the convent building except for occasional walks—two
hours each way, painful for her bad leg—to Mitaki, a
mountain where there were three beautiful waterfalls.

In time, she discovered she had surprising hardihood and tenacity, which she credited to all she had learned about herself in the hours and weeks after the bombing. When Mother Superior, Marie Saint-Jean de Kenti, asked her one day what she would do if she were told she had failed and would have to leave, she said, "I would take hold of that beam there and hold on with all my strength." She did hold on, and in 1957 she took vows of poverty, chastity, and obedience and became Sister Dominique Sasaki.

By now, the Society of Helpers knew her strength, and it assigned her, straight from the novitiate, to the post of director of a home for seventy old people near Kurosaki, on Kyushu, named the Garden of St. Joseph. She was only thirty-three, and she was the first Japanese director of the home—in command of a staff of fifteen, five of whom were French and Belgian nuns. She had to plunge straight into negotiations with local and national bureaucrats. She had no books to read on care of the aged. She inherited a decrepit wooden building—a former temple—and an institution that had had difficulty even feeding its enfeebled inmates, some of whom had had to be sent out foraging for firewood. Most of the old men were former coal miners from the notoriously cruel Kyushu mines. Some of the foreign nuns were crusty, and their modes of speech, unlike those of the Japanese, were blunt, harsh, and hurtful to Sister Sasaki.

The Aftermath

Her hard-earned doggedness told, and she remained fully in charge of the Garden of St. Joseph for twenty years. Thanks to her schooling as an accountant, she was able to introduce a rational system of bookkeeping. Eventually, the Society of Helpers, with support from branches in the United States, raised money for a new building, and Sister Sasaki supervised the construction of a concrete-block structure cut into the brow of a hill. A few years later, a subterranean waterway began to undermine it, and she saw to its replacement with a more modern building, of reinforced concrete, with single and double rooms fitted with Western-style washbasins and toilets.

Her greatest gift, she found, was her ability to help inmates to die in peace. She had seen so much death in Hiroshima after the bombing, and had seen what strange things so many people did when they were cornered by death, that nothing now surprised or frightened her. The first time she stood watch by a dying inmate, she vividly remembered a night soon after the bombing when she had lain out in the open, uncared for, in dreadful pain, beside a young man who was dying. She had talked with him all night, and had become aware, above all, of his fearful loneliness. She had watched him die in the morning. At deathbeds in the home, she was always mindful of this terrible solitude. She would speak little to the dying person but would hold a hand or touch an arm, as an assertion, simply, that she was there.

Once, an old man revealed to her on his deathbed,

with such vividness she felt she was witnessing the act, that he had stabbed another man in the back and had watched him bleed to death. Though the murderer was not a Christian, Sister Sasaki told him that God forgave him, and he died in comfort. Another old man had, like many Kyushu miners, been a drunkard. He had had a sordid reputation; his family had abandoned him. In the home, he tried with pathetic eagerness to please everyone. He volunteered to carry coal from storage bins, and he stoked the building's boiler. He had cirrhosis of the liver, and had been warned not to accept the daily ration of five ounces of distilled spirits that the Garden of St. Joseph mercifully issued to the former miners. But he continued to drink it. Vomiting at the supper table one night, he ruptured a blood vessel. It took him three days to die. Sister Sasaki stayed beside him all that time, holding his hand, so that he might die knowing that, living, he had pleased her.

In 1970, Sister Sasaki attended an international conference of working nuns in Rome and, after it, inspected welfare facilities in Italy, Switzerland, France, Belgium, and England. She retired from the Garden of St. Joseph at the age of fifty-five, in 1978, and was awarded a vacation trip to the Holy See. Unable to be idle, she installed herself at a table outside St. Peter's to give advice to Japanese tourists; later, she became a tourist herself, in Florence, Padua, Assisi, Venice, Milan, and Paris.

Back in Japan, she did volunteer work for two years at the Tokyo headquarters of the Society of Helpers,

The Aftermath

then spent two years as Mother Superior of the convent at Misasa, where she had taken her training. After that, she led a tranquil life as superintendent of the women's dormitory at the music school where her brother had studied; it had been taken over by the Church and was now called the Elizabeth College of Music. After finishing at the school, Yasuo had become qualified as a schoolteacher, and now he taught composition and mathematics in a high school in Kochi, on the island of Shikoku. Yaeko was married to a doctor who owned his own clinic in Hiroshima, and Sister Sasaki could go to him if she needed a doctor. Besides continuing difficulties with her leg, she had endured for some years a pattern of ailments which—as with so many hibakusha—might or might not have been attributable to the bomb: liver dysfunction, night sweats and morning fevers, borderline angina, blood spots on her legs, and signs in blood tests of a rheumatoid factor.

One of the happiest moments in her life came in 1980, while she was stationed at the society's headquarters in Tokyo: she was honored at a dinner to celebrate the twenty-fifth anniversary of her becoming a nun. By chance, a second guest of honor that night was the head of the society in Paris, Mother General France Delcourt, who, it happened, had also reached her twenty-fifth year in the order. Mother Delcourt gave Sister Sasaki a present of a picture of the Virgin Mary. Sister Sasaki made a speech: "I shall not dwell on the past. It is as if I had been given a spare life when I survived the A-bomb. But I prefer not to look back. I shall keep moving forward."

5 · DR. MASAKAZU FUJII

A CONVIVIAL MAN, fifty years old, Dr. Fujii enjoyed the company of foreigners, and as his practice in the Kaitaichi clinic rolled comfortably along, it was his pleasure, in the evenings, to ply members of the occupying forces with a seemingly endless supply of Suntory whiskey that he somehow laid hands on. For years he had had a hobby of studying foreign languages, English among them. Father Kleinsorge had long been a friend, and he used to visit in the evenings to teach Dr. Fujii to speak German. The doctor had also taken up Esperanto. During the war the Japanese secret police had got it into their heads that the Russians used Esperanto for their spying codes, and Dr. Fujii had more than once been questioned closely about whether he was getting messages from the Comintern. He was now eager to make friends with Americans.

In 1948, he built a new clinic, in Hiroshima, on the site of the one that had been ruined by the bomb. The new one was a modest wooden building with half a dozen bedrooms for in-patients. He had trained as an orthopedic surgeon, but after the war that craft was becoming subdivided into various specialties. He had earlier had as a special interest prenatal hip dislocations, but he now thought himself too old to go very far with that or

The Aftermath

any other specialty; besides, he lacked the sophisticated equipment needed for specialization. He performed operations on keloids, did appendectomies, and treated wounds; he also took medical (and, occasionally, venereal) cases. Through his Occupation friends, he was able to get penicillin. He treated about eighty patients a day.

He had five grown children, and, in the Japanese tradition, they followed in their father's footsteps. The oldest and youngest were daughters, Myeko and Chieko, and both married doctors. The oldest son, Masatoshi, a doctor, inherited the Kaitaichi clinic and its practice; the second son, Keiji, did not go to medical school but became an X-ray technician; and the third son, Shigeyuki, was a young doctor on the staff of the Nihon University Hospital in Tokyo. Keiji lived with his parents, in a house that Dr. Fujii had built next to the Hiroshima clinic.

DR. FUJII suffered from none of the effects of radiation overdose, and he evidently felt that for any psychological damage the horrors of the bombing may have done him the best therapy was to follow the pleasure principle. Indeed, he recommended to hibakusha who did have radiation symptoms that they take a regular dosage of alcohol. He enjoyed himself. He was compassionate toward his patients, but he did not believe in working too hard. He had a dance floor installed in his house. He bought a billiard table. He enjoyed photography and built himself a darkroom. He played mah-jongg. He loved having foreign houseguests. At bedtime, his nurses gave him massages and, sometimes, therapeutic injections.

He took up golf, and built a sand bunker and set up a driving net in his garden. In 1955, he paid the entrance fee of a hundred and fifty thousand yen, then a little more than four hundred dollars, to join the exclusive Hiroshima Country Club. He did not play much golf, but, to the eventual great joy of his children, he kept the family membership. Thirty years later, it would cost fifteen million yen, or sixty thousand dollars, to join the club.

He succumbed to the Japanese baseball mania. The Hiroshima players were at first called, in English, the Carps, until he pointed out to the public that the plural for that fish, and for those ballplayers, had no "s." He went often to watch games at the huge new stadium, not far from the A-Bomb Dome—the ruins of the Hiroshima Industrial Promotion Hall, which the city had kept as its only direct physical reminder of the bomb. In their early seasons, the Carp had dismal records, yet they had a fanatical following, something like those of the Brooklyn Dodgers and the New York Mets in their lean years. But Dr. Fujii rather mischievously rooted for the Tokyo Swallows; he wore a Swallows button on the lapel of his jacket.

Hiroshima, in its regeneration as a brand-new city after the bombing, turned up with one of the gaudiest entertainment districts in all Japan—an area where, at night, vast neon signs of many colors winked and beckoned to potential customers of bars, geisha houses, coffee shops, dance halls, and licensed houses of prostitution. One night, Dr. Fujii, who had begun to have a reputation as a *purayboy*, or playboy, took his tenderfoot son Shigeyuki, who was twenty years old and home awhile from the grind of his Tokyo medical school, out on the town to show him how to be a man. They went to a building where there was a huge dance floor, with girls lined up along one side. Shigeyuki told his father he didn't know what to do; his legs felt weak. Dr. Fujii bought a ticket, picked out an especially beautiful girl, and told Shigeyuki to bow to her and take her out there and do the step that he had taught him on the dance floor at home. He told the girl to be gentle with his son, and he drifted away.

In 1956, Dr. Fujii had an adventure. At the time the so-called Hiroshima Maidens had gone to the United States for plastic surgery, the year before, they were accompanied by two Hiroshima surgeons. Those two could not stay away for more than a year, and Dr. Fujii was selected to take the place of one of them. He left in February, and for ten months, in and around New York, he played the part of a warm and caring father to twenty-five handicapped daughters. He observed their operations at Mount Sinai Hospital and acted as interpreter between the American doctors and the girls, helping the latter to understand what was happening to them. It pleased him to be able to speak German with the Jewish wives of some of the doctors, and at one reception no less a person than the governor of New York State complimented him on his English.

The girls, staying with American host families who

spoke little or no Japanese, were often lonely, and Dr. Fujii devised ways to cheer them up. He was playful and considerate. He organized outings for Japanese food, taking two or three girls at a time. Once, a party was to be given by an American doctor and his wife just three days after one of the Maidens, Michiko Yamaoka, had undergone a major operation. Her face had a dressing on it, and her hands were bandaged and strapped to her body. Dr. Fujii didn't want her to miss the party, and he got one of the American doctors to arrange for her to ride through the city to the party in an open red limousine, behind a police escort with a siren. On the way, Dr. Fujii had them stop at a drugstore, where he bought Michiko a toy horse for ten cents; he asked the policeman to take a picture of the presentation of this gift.

Sometimes, he went out alone to have a good time. The other Japanese doctor, named Takahashi, was his hotel roommate. Dr. Takahashi was a light drinker and a light sleeper. Late at night, Dr. Fujii would come in, crash around, flop down, and break into a sleep-shattering symphony of snores. He was having a wonderful time.

WAS he, nine years later, in Hiroshima, still so happy-go-lucky? His daughter Chieko's husband thought not. The son-in-law thought he saw signs of a growing stubbornness and rigidity in him, and a turn toward melancholy. So that Dr. Fujii could ease up in his work, his third son, Shigeyuki, gave up his practice in Tokyo and came to be his assistant, moving into a house that his father had built on a plot of ground about a block from the clinic. One cloud in the father's life was a quarrel in the Hiroshima Lions Club, of which he was president. The fight was over whether the club should try, through its admissions policy, to become an exclusive, high-society organization, like some of the Japanese doctors' associations, or remain essentially a service organization, open to all. When it appeared that Dr. Fujii might lose out in his fight for the latter view, he abruptly and disappointedly resigned.

His relationship with his wife was growing difficult. Ever since his trip to America, he had wanted a house like that of one of the Mount Sinai doctors, and now, to her chagrin, he designed and built, next to the wooden house Shigeyuki was living in, a three-story concrete home for himself alone. On the ground floor it had a living room and an American-style kitchen; his study was on the second floor, lined with bound books, which Shigeyuki eventually found to be volume after volume of meticulous copies he had made in medical school of course notes by a classmate named Iwamoto, who was brighter than he; and on the top floor were an eight-mat Japanese-style bedroom and an American-style bathroom.

Toward the end of 1963, he rushed its completion, so it would be ready to house an American couple who had been host parents to some Maidens and were coming to visit after the first of the year. He wanted to sleep there for a few nights to try it out. His wife argued against the haste, but he stubbornly moved in, late in December.

NEW YEAR'S EVE, 1963. Dr. Fujii sat cozily on the tatami matting of Shigeyuki's living room with his legs in a *kotatsu*, an electrically heated foot-warming recess in the floor. Also gathered there were Shigeyuki and his wife and another couple, but not Dr. Fujii's wife. The plan was to have some drinks and watch an annual New Year's Eve television program called "Ko-haku Uta-Gassen," a contest between red (female) and white (male) teams of popular singers who had been chosen for the program by a poll of listeners; judges were famous actresses, authors, golfers, baseball players. The program would run from nine to eleven-forty-five, and then there would be bell ringing for the New Year. At about eleven, Shigeyuki noticed that his father, who had not been drinking much, was nodding, and suggested that he go off to bed. And in a few minutes, before the end of the program, he did—this time without the ministrations of a nurse who, most nights, massaged his legs and tucked him in. After a while, worrying about his father, Shigeyuki went out and around to the river side of the new house, where, looking up, he saw a light burning in the bedroom window. He thought all was well.

The family had made a plan to meet the next morning at eleven for drinks and the traditional New Year's breakfast of *ozoni*, a soup, and *mochi*, rice cakes. Chieko and her husband and some other guests arrived and began drinking. At half past eleven, Dr. Fujii had not appeared, and Shigeyuki sent his seven-year-old son, Masatsugu, out to call up to his window. The boy, getting no answer, tried the door. It was locked. He borrowed a ladder from a neighbor's house and climbed to the top of it to call some more, and still there was no response. When he told his parents, they became alarmed and hurried out, broke a window next to the locked door to get it open, and, smelling gas, rushed upstairs. There they found Dr. Fujii unconscious, with a gas heater at the head of his futon turned on but not burning. Strangely, a ventilator fan was also turned on; the draft of fresh air from it had probably kept him alive. He was stretched out on his back, looking serene.

There were three doctors present—son, son-in-law, and a guest—and, fetching oxygen and other equipment from the clinic, they did everything they could to revive Dr. Fujii. They called in one of the best doctors they knew, a Professor Myanishi, from Hiroshima University. His first question: "Was this a suicide attempt?" The family thought not. There was nothing to be done until January 4th; everything in Hiroshima would be shut down tight for the three-day New Year's holiday, and hospital services would be at a minimum. Dr. Fujii remained unconscious, but his life signs seemed not to be critical. On the fourth, an ambulance came. As the bearers were carrying Dr. Fujii downstairs, he stirred. Swimming up toward consciousness, he apparently thought he was being rescued, somehow, after the atomic bombing. "Who are you?" he asked the bearers. "Are you soldiers?"

In the university hospital, he began to recover. On January 15th, when the annual sumo wrestling contests began, he asked for the portable television set he had bought in America, and he sat up in bed watching. He could feed himself, though his handling of chopsticks was a bit awkward. He asked for a bottle of *sake*.

By now, everyone in the family was off guard. On January 25th, his stool was suddenly watery and bloody, and he became dehydrated and lost consciousness.

For the next eleven years, he lived the life of a vegetable. He remained in the hospital, fed through a tube, for two and a half years, and then was taken home, where his wife and a loyal servant cared for him, feeding him through the tube, changing his diapers, bathing him, massaging him, medicating him for urinary infections he developed. At times, he seemed to respond to voices, and sometimes he seemed to be dimly registering pleasure or displeasure.

At ten o'clock on the night of January 11, 1973, Shigeyuki took his son Masatsugu, the boy who had climbed the ladder to call his grandfather on the day of the accident, now a premedical student of sixteen, to Dr. Fujii's bedside. He wanted the boy to see his grandfather with the eye of a doctor. Masatsugu listened to his grandfather's breathing and heartbeat and took his blood pressure; he judged his condition stable, and Shigeyuki agreed.

The next morning, Shigeyuki's mother telephoned him, saying that his father looked funny to her. When Shigeyuki arrived, Dr. Fujii was dead.

The doctor's widow was against having an autopsy done. Shigeyuki wanted one, and he resorted to a ruse. He had the body taken to a crematorium; then, that night, it was taken out a back way and was delivered to the American-run Atomic Bomb Casualty Commission, on top of a hill to the east of the city. When the post mortem had been done, Shigeyuki went for the report. Finding his father's organs distributed in various containers, he had the strangest feeling of a last encounter, and he said, "There you are, *Oto-chan*—there you are, Papa." He was shown that his father's brain had atrophied, his large intestine had become enlarged, and there was a cancer the size of a Ping-Pong ball in his liver.

The remains were cremated and buried in the grounds of the Night of the Lotus Temple, of the Jodo Shinshu sect of Buddhism, near his maternal family home in Nagatsuka.

THEN came a sad ending to this hibakusha's story. His family quarrelled over his property, and a mother sued a son.

6 · KIYOSHI TANIMOTO

A YEAR AFTER the bombing, Hiroshimans had begun repossessing the plots of rubble where their houses had once stood. Many had built crude wooden huts, having scavenged fallen tiles from ruins to make their roofs. There was no electricity to light their shacks, and at dusk each evening, lonely, confused, and disillusioned, they gathered in an open area near the Yokogawa railroad station to deal in the black markets and console each other. Into this zone now trooped, each evening, Kiyoshi Tanimoto and four other Protestant ministers and, with them, a trumpeter and a drummer tooting and thumping "Onward, Christian Soldiers." Taking turns, the ministers stood on a box and preached. With so little to entertain them, a crowd always gathered, even including some *panpan* girls, as prostitutes who catered to GIs came to be called. The anger of many hibakusha, directed at first against the Americans for dropping the bomb, had by now subtly modulated toward their own government, for having involved the country in a rash and doomed aggression. The preachers said that it was no use blaming the government; that the hope of the Japanese people lay in repenting their sinful past and relying on God: "Seek ye first the Kingdom of God, and His righteousness; and all these things shall be added unto you. Take therefore no thought for the morrow: for the morrow shall take thought for the things of itself. Sufficient unto the day is the evil thereof."

Because he had no church into which to lure converts, if there should be any, Kiyoshi Tanimoto soon realized the futility of this evangelism. Parts of the reinforced-concrete shell of his Gothic-towered church in the city still stood, and he now turned his mind to trying to find ways to restore the building. He had no money. The building had been insured for a hundred and fifty thousand yen, then less than five hundred dollars, but bank

The Aftermath

funds had been frozen by the conquerors. Learning that military supplies were being allocated for various kinds of reconstruction, he got requisition slips for "conversion materials" from the prefectural government and began a hunt for things he could use or sell. In that time of widespread thievery and of resentment of the Japanese military, many of the supply depots had been looted. Finally, he found on the island of Kamagari a warehouse of paints. American Occupation personnel had made a mess of the place. Unable to read Japanese labels, they had punctured many cans and kicked them over, apparently to see what was in them. The minister got hold of a boat and carried a big cargo of empty cans to the mainland, and he was able to barter them with an outfit named the Toda Construction Company for a tile roof for his church. Little by little, over the months, he and a few loyal parishioners worked on the carpentry for the building with their own hands, but they lacked the funds to do much.

ON July 1, 1946, *before the first anniversary of the bombing, the United States had tested an atomic bomb at the Bikini Atoll. On May 17, 1948, the Americans announced the successful completion of another test.*

IN correspondence with an Emory University classmate, the Reverend Mr. Marvin Green, who was now pastor of the Park Church in Weehawken, New Jersey, Kiyoshi Tanimoto told of his difficulties in restoring his church. Green arranged with the Methodist Board of Missions

175

an invitation to Tanimoto to visit the United States to raise money, and in October, 1948, Tanimoto, leaving his family behind, embarked for San Francisco on an American transport, the U.S.S. *Gordon*.

On the sea voyage, an ambitious idea grew in his mind. He would spend his life working for peace. He was becoming convinced that the collective memory of the hibakusha would be a potent force for peace in the world, and that there ought to be in Hiroshima a center where the experience of the bombing could become the focus of international studies of means to assure that atomic weapons would never be used again. Eventually, in the States, without thinking to check with Mayor Shinzo Hamai or anyone else in Hiroshima, he drafted a memorandum sketching this idea.

He lived as a guest in the basement of Marvin Green's Weehawken parsonage. The Reverend Mr. Green, enlisting the help of some volunteers, became his manager and promoter. From a church directory he compiled a list of all the churches in the country with more than two hundred members or with budgets of more than twenty thousand dollars, and to hundreds of these he sent out hand-done broadsides soliciting invitations for Kiyoshi Tanimoto to lecture. He drew up a series of itineraries, and soon Tanimoto was on the road with a set speech, "The Faith That Grew Out of the Ashes." At each church, a collection was taken.

On and between speaking trips, Tanimoto began submitting his peace-center memorandum to people he hoped might be influential. On one visit to New York from Weehawken, he was taken by a Japanese friend of his to meet Pearl Buck, in the office of her husband's publishing firm. She read, and he explained, his memorandum. She said she was impressed by the proposal, but she felt she was too old and too busy to help him. She thought, however, that she knew just the person who might: Norman Cousins, the editor of *The Saturday Review of Literature*. Mr. Tanimoto should send his memo to Mr. Cousins, and she would speak to him about it.

One day not long afterward, while the minister was touring a rural area near Atlanta with his lecture, he got a telephone call from Cousins, who said he was deeply moved by the memorandum—might he put it in the *Saturday Review* as a guest editorial?

On March 5, 1949, the memorandum appeared in the magazine, under the title "Hiroshima's Idea"—an idea that, Cousins' introductory note said, "the editors enthusiastically endorse and with which they will associate themselves":

> The people of Hiroshima, aroused from the daze that followed the atomic bombing of their city on August 6, 1945, know themselves to have been part of a laboratory experiment which proved the long-time thesis of peacemakers. Almost to a man, they have accepted as a compelling responsibility their mission to help in preventing further similar destruction anywhere in the world. . . .

HIROSHIMA

The people of Hiroshima . . . earnestly desire that out of their experience there may develop some permanent contribution to the cause of world peace. Towards this end, we propose the establishment of a World Peace Center, international and nonsectarian, which will serve as a laboratory of research and planning for peace education throughout the world. . . .

The people of Hiroshima were in fact, to a man, totally unaware of Kiyoshi Tanimoto's (and now Norman Cousins') proposal. They were, nonetheless, acutely aware of the special role that the city was destined to play in the world's memory. On August 6th, the fourth anniversary of the bombing, the national Diet promulgated a law establishing Hiroshima as a Peace Memorial City, and the final design for the commemorative park by the great Japanese architect Kenzo Tange was revealed to the public. At the heart of the park, there would be, in memory of those who had died, a solemn cenotaph in the shape of a *haniwa*, an arch of clay, presumably a house for the dead, found in prehistoric tombs in Japan. A large crowd gathered for the annual Peace Memorial Ceremony. Tanimoto was far away from all this, touring American churches.

A few days after the anniversary, Norman Cousins visited Hiroshima. Kiyoshi Tanimoto's idea had been pushed aside in Cousins' mind by a new one, of his own: that an international petition in support of the United World Federalists—a group urging world government—

should be submitted to President Truman, who had ordered the dropping of the bomb. Within a short time, 107,854 signatures had been gathered in the city. After a visit to an orphanage, Cousins returned to the States with yet another idea—for "moral adoption" of Hiroshima orphans by Americans, who would send financial support for the children. Signatures for the World Federalist petition were being gathered in the United States as well, and Cousins thrilled Tanimoto, who until then had known very little about the organization, by inviting him to be in the delegation that would present the petition to President Truman.

Unfortunately, Harry Truman declined to receive the petitioners and refused to accept the petition.

O*N September 23, 1949, Moscow Radio announced that the Soviet Union had developed an atomic bomb.*

B*Y* the end of the year, Kiyoshi Tanimoto had visited two hundred and fifty-six cities, in thirty-one states, and had raised about ten thousand dollars for his church. Before he left for home, Marvin Green happened to mention that he was about to give up on his old green Cadillac. His friend Tani asked him to donate it to the church in Hiroshima, and he did. Through a Japanese acquaintance in the shipping business, Tanimoto arranged to have it transported free of charge to Japan.

Back home at the beginning of 1950, Tanimoto called on Mayor Hamai and the Prefectural Governor, Tsunei Kusunose, asking their official support for his peace-center idea. They turned him down. Through a press code and other measures, General Douglas MacArthur, the supreme commander of the occupying forces, had strictly prohibited dissemination of or agitation for any reports on the consequences of the Hiroshima and Nagasaki bombings—including the consequence of a desire for peace—and the officials evidently thought that Tanimoto's peace center might get the local governments in trouble. Tanimoto persevered, calling together a number of leading citizens, and, after Norman Cousins had set up a Hiroshima Peace Center Foundation in New York to receive American funds, these people established the center in Hiroshima, with Tanimoto's church as its base. At first, it found little to do. (Only years later, when a Peace Memorial Museum and Peace Memorial Hall had been built in the park, and lively—and sometimes turbulent—annual international conferences on peace issues were taking place in the city, could Kiyoshi Tanimoto's early planting of seeds for these things, and his courage in ignoring the MacArthur restraints, be acknowledged by at least some Hiroshimans.)

The Cadillac arrived, and the jubilant minister decided to take the gas guzzler for a spin. As he was climbing the heights of Hijiyama, to the east of the city, he was stopped by a policeman and arrested for driving without a license. It happened that he had recently begun serving as chaplain of the police academy, and when the higher-ups at the police station saw him brought in they laughed and let him go.

. . .

The Aftermath

In midsummer of 1950, Cousins invited Tanimoto to return to the United States for a second tour, to raise money for the World Federalists, for moral adoption, and for the peace center, and late in August Tanimoto was off again. Marvin Green arranged things, as before. This time, Tanimoto visited two hundred and one cities, in twenty-four states, over eight months. The high point of the trip (and possibly of his life) was a visit to Washington, arranged by Cousins, where, on February 5, 1951, after having lunch with members of the House Foreign Affairs Committee, he gave the opening prayer for the afternoon session of the Senate:

> Our Heavenly Father, we thank Thee for the great blessing Thou hast granted America in enabling her to build in this last decade the greatest civilization in human history. . . . We thank Thee, God, that Japan has been permitted to be one of the fortunate recipients of American generosity. We thank Thee that our people have been given the gift of freedom, enabling them to rise from the ashes of ruin and be reborn. . . . God bless all members of this Senate. . . .

Virginia's Senator A. Willis Robertson rose and declared himself "dumbfounded yet inspired" that a man "whom we tried to kill with an atomic bomb came to the Senate floor and, offering up thanks to the same God we worship, thanked Him for America's great spiritual heritage, and then asked God to bless every member of the Senate."

THE DAY before the bomb was dropped on Hiroshima, the city, in fear of incendiary raids, had put hundreds of schoolgirls to work helping to tear down houses and clear fire lanes. They were out in the open when the bomb exploded. Few survived. Of those who did, many suffered bad burns and later developed ugly keloids on their faces, arms, and hands. A month after Tanimoto returned from his second trip to the States, he started, as a project of his peace center, a Bible class for about a dozen of them—the Society of Keloid Girls, he called them. He bought three sewing machines and put the girls to work in a dressmaking workshop on the second floor of another of his projects, a warwidows' home he had founded. He asked the city government for funds for plastic surgery for the Keloid Girls. It turned him down. He then applied to the Atomic Bomb Casualty Commission, which had been set up to study the radiation aftereffects of the bomb—aftereffects that those who made the decision to drop the bomb had utterly failed to foresee. The A.B.C.C. reminded him that it carried on research, not treatment. (The A.B.C.C. was keenly resented for this reason by hibakusha; they said that the Americans regarded them as laboratory guinea pigs or rats.)

A woman named Shizue Masugi now visited Hiroshima from Tokyo. She had led a wildly unconventional life for a Japanese woman of her time. A journalist, married and divorced while young, she had later been the mistress, in turn, of two famous novelists and, later still, had married again. She had written short stories about the bitter loves and bitter solitude of women and was now writing a column for lovelorn women in the big Tokyo newspaper *Yomiuri Shimbun*. She would become a Catholic before she died, but she would choose to be buried in the Tokeiji Temple, a Zen center founded in 1285 by a monk who felt sorry for women with cruel husbands and decreed that any of them who took asylum in his temple as nuns could consider themselves divorced. On her trip to Hiroshima, she asked Kiyoshi Tanimoto what most needed to be done for women who were hibakusha. He suggested plastic surgery for the Keloid Girls. She started a campaign for funds in the *Yomiuri*, and soon nine girls were taken to Tokyo for surgery. Later, twelve more were taken to Osaka. Newspapers called them, to their chagrin, *Genbaku Otome*, a phrase that was translated into English, literally, as A-Bomb Maidens.

IN October 1952, Great Britain conducted its first test of an atomic bomb and the United States its first of a hydrogen bomb. In August 1953, the Soviet Union also tested a hydrogen bomb.

THE Tokyo and Osaka operations on the girls were not altogether successful, and, on a visit to Hiroshima, Kiyoshi Tanimoto's friend Marvin Green wondered whether it might be possible for some of them to be taken to America, where the techniques of plastic surgery were more advanced. In September 1953, Norman Cousins arrived in Hiroshima with his wife to deliver some moral-adoption funds. Tanimoto introduced them to a few of the girls, and spoke of Marvin Green's idea. They liked it.

After their departure, an awkward meeting took place in the Mayor's office, at which distribution to orphans of the moral-adoption funds was discussed. Cousins had brought fifteen hundred dollars, but it turned out that two hundred dollars of this amount had been set aside for six particular children, sixty-five dollars had been allocated to the Maidens, and a hundred and nineteen dollars had been spent by Tanimoto at the Fukuya department store for briefcases to be presented as gifts by Norman Cousins to the directors of six orphanages. This left eleven hundred and sixty-five dollars, or only about two dollars and seventy cents for each of four hundred and ten orphans. The city officials, who thought they were in charge of the project, were furious about the sums Tanimoto had deducted. In a report of this meeting, the Hiroshima paper *Chugoku Shimbun* reported, "Rev. Tanimoto responded, 'I was following Mr. Cousins's instructions in this, not my own wishes.'"

Tanimoto had lately been getting used to criticism. His long absences from his church for trips to America had earned him the nickname of A-bomb minister. Hi-

The Aftermath

roshima doctors had wanted to know why the Maidens were not operated on in Hiroshima. And why just girls? Why not boys? Some people thought they saw the Reverend Mr. Tanimoto's name in the paper too often. The enormous Cadillac had not gone down well, even though it had quickly turned out to be a dog and had had to be junked.

ON *March 1, 1954, the Lucky Dragon No. 5 was showered with radioactive fallout from an American test at Bikini Atoll.*

NORMAN COUSINS had gone to work in New York on the Maidens idea, and in late 1954 Dr. Arthur Barsky, the chief of plastic surgery at both Mount Sinai and Beth Israel hospitals, and Dr. William Hitzig, an internist on the Mount Sinai staff and Cousins' personal physician, arrived in Hiroshima to cull from among the Maidens those whose prospects for transformation by surgery were best. Of the many disfigured girls in the city, only forty-three presented themselves to be examined. The doctors chose twenty-five.

On May 5, 1955, Kiyoshi Tanimoto took off with the girls from Iwakuni Airport in a United States Military Air Transport plane. As the girls were being settled in host homes around New York, he was hustled off to the West Coast for the start of yet another fund-raising tour. Among other appointments on his itinerary was one for the evening of Wednesday, May 11th, at the NBC studios in Los Angeles, for what Cousins gave him to understand would be a local television interview that would be helpful to the project.

That evening, somewhat fuddled, he was seated before bright lights and cameras on a living-room–like set. An American gentleman he had just met, named Ralph Edwards, beamed and, turning to the camera, addressed an estimated forty million Americans he attracted every Wednesday night: "Good evening, ladies and gentlemen, and welcome to 'This Is Your Life.' The ticking you hear in the background is a clock counting off the seconds to 8:15 A.M., August 6, 1945. And seated here with me is a gentleman whose life was changed by the last tick of that clock as it reached eight-fifteen. Good evening, sir. Would you tell us your name?"

"Kiyoshi Tanimoto."

"And what is your occupation?"

"I am a minister."

"And where is your home?"

"Hiroshima, Japan."

"And where were you on August 6, 1945, at eight-fifteen in the morning?"

Tanimoto had no chance to answer. The ticking grew louder and louder, and there was an uproar from kettle-drums.

"*This* is Hiroshima," Edwards said as a mushroom cloud grew on the viewers' screens, "and in that fateful second on August 6, 1945, a new concept of life and death was given its baptism. And tonight's principal subject—you, Reverend Tanimoto!—were an unsuspecting part of that

The Aftermath

concept. . . . We will pick up the threads of your life in a moment, Reverend Tanimoto, after this word from Bob Warren, our announcer, who has something very special to say to the girls in the audience."

The fateful clock of doom, now unheard, ticked off sixty additional seconds as Bob Warren tried to remove Hazel Bishop nail polish from a blonde's fingernails— an effort that was unsuccessful, even though he resorted to using a metal scouring pad, with which he had succeeded in removing rust from a frying pan.

Kiyoshi Tanimoto was totally unprepared for what followed. He sat there, torpid, sweating, and tongue-tied, as, after the manner of the famous program, his life was sketchily reviewed. Through an archway came Miss Bertha Sparkey, an elderly Methodist missionary who had taught him in his youth about Christ. Then came his friend Marvin Green, with a joke about life in divinity school. Then Edwards pointed out in the studio audience some parishioners Tanimoto had had just after his ordination, during a brief temporary pastorate in the Japanese-American Hollywood Independence Church.

Next came the shocker. In walked a tall, fattish American man, whom Edwards introduced as Captain Robert Lewis, copilot of the *Enola Gay* on the Hiroshima mission. In a shaky voice, Lewis told about the flight. Tanimoto sat there with a face of wood. At one point, Lewis broke off, closed his eyes, and rubbed his forehead, and forty million watchers across the land must have thought he was crying. (He was not. He had been drinking. Years

187

later, Marvin Green told a young journalist named Rod-
ney Barker, who was writing a book on the Maidens,
that Lewis had panicked the show people by failing to
turn up that afternoon for the rehearsal of all the par-
ticipants except Tanimoto. It seemed that he had expected to be given a fat check for appearing on the show,
and when he learned that he would not, he had gone
out bar crawling. Green said he had found the copilot
in time to get a cup of coffee in him before the show.)

Edwards: "Did you write something in your log at that
time?"

Lewis: "I wrote down the words, 'My God, what have
we done?' "

After that, Chisa Tanimoto trotted onstage with clipped
steps, because she was wearing what she never wore at
home—a kimono. In Hiroshima, she had been given two
days to uproot herself—and the four children she and
her husband now had—and get to Los Angeles. There
they had all been incarcerated in a hotel, kept strictly
away from their husband and father. For the first time
on the show, Tanimoto's expression changed—to surprise; he seemed to have become a stranger to pleasure.
Next, two of the Maidens, Toyoko Minowa and Tadako
Emori, were presented in silhouette behind a translucent
screen, and Edwards made a pitch to the audience for
money for the Maidens' operations. And, finally, the
four Tanimoto children—daughter Koko, who had been
an infant in the bombing, now ten; son Ken, seven;
daughter Jun, four; and son Shin, two—came running
out into their father's arms.

The Aftermath

FROM: TOKYO
TO: SECRETARY OF STATE

MAY 12, 1955

EMBASSY-USIS SHARE WASHINGTON CONCERN LEST HIROSHIMA GIRLS PROJECT GENERATE UNFAVORABLE PUBLICITY....

TANIMOTO IS LOOKED UPON HERE AS SOMETHING OF A PUBLICITY SEEKER. MAY WELL TRY TO TAKE ADVANTAGE OF TRIP TO RAISE FUNDS FOR HIROSHIMA MEMORIAL PEACE CENTER, HIS PET PROJECT. DO NOT BELIEVE HE IS RED OR RED-SYMPATHIZER, BUT HE CAN EASILY BECOME SOURCE OF MISCHIEVOUS PUBLICITY....

By diplomatic pouch:

SECRET

The Reverend Tanimoto is pictured as one who appears to be anti-Communist and probably sincere in his efforts to assist the girls.... However, in his desire to enhance his own prestige and importance he might ignorantly, innocently, or purposefully lend himself to or pursue a leftist line....

RALPH J. BLAKE
AMERICAN CONSUL GENERAL, KOBE

Upon getting back East after the show, Robert Lewis, who had resigned from the Air Force and was working as personnel manager of Henry Heide, candy makers, in New York, was called to the Pentagon and given a heavy chewing out by the Defense Department.

The whole Tanimoto family remained in the United States through the rest of Kiyoshi's speaking tour, which took him to a total of a hundred and ninety-five cities, in twenty-six states. The television show had brought in about fifty thousand dollars, and he raised ten thousand more. Chisa Tanimoto and the children stayed through a glorious summer in a guesthouse on Pearl Buck's farm in Bucks County, Pennsylvania.

On August 6th, the tenth anniversary of the Hiroshima bombing, Tanimoto placed a wreath on the Tomb of the Unknown Soldier at Arlington National Cemetery. On that day, in Hiroshima itself, far away from him, a genuine Japanese peace movement, riding the anger over the *Lucky Dragon* incident, got under way. Five thousand delegates attended the first World Conference against Atomic and Hydrogen Bombs.

The Tanimotos returned to Japan in December.

Kiyoshi Tanimoto had been swept out of the mainstream into an eddy. On his American speaking tours, he had displayed an energy that was remarkable for a hibakusha, speaking night after night after night on the weary circuits. But the reality was that for some years now he had been hurled along on the white water of Norman Cousins' ferocious energy. Cousins had given him heady experiences that fed his vanity, but he had also now taken out of the minister's hands the control of his own undertakings. Tanimoto had started the whole effort for the Maidens, but he discovered that even though the money raised by "This Is Your Life" would pay the Maidens' expenses, all but one thousand dollars of the money he had raised on his tour was also to be controlled by New York. Cousins had bypassed the peace center in Hiroshima and dealt with the city government; Tanimoto had begged to have the moral-adoption project put under the center's wing, but his role had turned out to be that of a shopper for briefcases. The crowning blow came when the ashes of the Maiden named Tomoko Nakabayashi, who had died under anaesthesia at Mount Sinai, were returned to her parents in Hiroshima and he was not even invited to the funeral, which was conducted by his old friend Father Kleinsorge. And when all the Maidens had come home and, astonishingly, found themselves the objects not only of public curiosity but also of envy and spite, they resisted his publicity-minded efforts to form them into a "Zion Club," and fell away from him.

Nor did he have any place in the Japanese peace movement, for he had been out of the country at crucial moments in its development, and, besides, his Christian outlook made him suspicious of the radical groups that were on the cutting edge of antinuclear activity. While he was away on this last trip, a national organization called Nihon Gensuikyo, the Japan Council against Atomic and Hydrogen Bombs, had come into being, and there had been a surge of activity pushing the Diet for medical care for hibakusha. Like many hibakusha, he was repelled by the growing political coloration of these doings, and he stayed away from the mass meetings in Peace Park on the subsequent anniversaries.

On May 15, 1957, Great Britain conducted its first hydrogen-bomb test, on Christmas Island, in the Indian Ocean.

Koko, the daughter who as an infant had experienced the bombing, had been taken almost every year to the American-run A.B.C.C. for a physical checkup. On the whole, her health had been all right, although, like many hibakusha who had been babies at the time of the bombing, her growth was definitely stunted. Now, an adolescent in junior high school, she went again. As usual, she undressed in a cubicle and put on a white hospital gown. When she had finished going through a battery of tests, this time she was taken into a brightly lit room where there was a low stage, backed by a wall marked with a measurement grid. She was stood against the wall, with lights in her eyes so glaring she could not see beyond them; she could hear Japanese and American voices. One of the former told her to take off the gown. She obeyed, and stood there for what seemed an eternity, with tears streaming down her face.

Koko was so frightened and hurt by this experience

that she was unable to tell anyone about it for twenty-five years.

ONE day toward the end of August, 1959, a baby girl was left in a basket in front of the altar of Kiyoshi Tanimoto's church. A note attached to its diaper gave the baby's name, Kanae, and its birth date, April 28th, and went on to say, "I am afraid I can't keep her at the moment. God bless her, and will you look after her in my stead?"

In the summer on Pearl Buck's farm, the Tanimoto children had played with the dozen orphans, mostly Oriental, that the American author had taken under her wing. The family had been impressed by Mrs. Buck's generosity, and now they decided to keep and raise the child who had been entrusted to them.

ON *February 13, 1960, France tested a nuclear weapon in the Sahara. On October 16, 1964, China carried out its first nuclear test, and on June 17, 1967, it exploded a hydrogen bomb.*

KOKO went to the States with her father in 1968, to enter the Centenary College for Women, in Hackettstown, New Jersey. Tanimoto had previously been back to America in 1964–65, when he visited his alma mater, Emory University, and then travelled home by way of Europe; and in 1966, when he received an honorary degree from Lewis and Clark College. Koko eventually transferred to American University, in Washington, D.C. There she fell in love with a Chinese-American and became engaged to marry him, but her fiancé's father, a doctor, said that because she had been exposed to the atomic bomb she couldn't bear a normal child, and he forbade the marriage.

Back in Japan, Koko took a job in Tokyo, working for an oil-drilling firm, Odeco. She told no one she was a hibakusha. In time, she found someone she could confide in—her boyfriend's best friend. He turned out, in the end, to be the man she married. She had a miscarriage, which she and her family attributed to the bomb. She and her husband went to the A.B.C.C. to have their chromosomes checked, and though nothing abnormal was found they decided not to try again to have a child. In time, they adopted two babies.

THE Japanese antinuclear movement had begun to split up in the early sixties. Gensuikyo, the Japan Council, was dominated at first by the Japanese Socialist Party and by Sohyo, the General Council of Trade Unions. In 1960, it had tried to block revision of the United States–Japanese Security Treaty, on the ground that it encouraged a renewed militarism in Japan, whereupon some more conservative groups formed Kakkin Kaigi, the National Council for Peace and against Nuclear Weapons. In 1964, a deeper division came about, when Communist infiltration of Gensuikyo caused the Socialists and the trade unions to pull out and form Gensuikin, the Japan Congress against Atomic and Hydrogen Bombs. For

The Aftermath

Tanimoto, as for most hibakusha, these quarrels reached the zenith of absurdity when Gensuikin argued that all nations should stop testing, while Gensuikyo argued that the United States was testing to prepare for war and the Soviet Union was testing to insure peace. The division persisted, and year after year the two organizations held separate conferences on August 6th. On June 7, 1973, Kiyoshi Tanimoto wrote the "Evening Essay" column in the Hiroshima *Chugoku Shimbun*:

> These last few years when August 6th approaches, voices are heard lamenting that this year, once again, the commemorative events will be held by a divided peace movement. . . . The sentence inscribed on the memorial Cenotaph—"Rest in peace, for the mistake shall not be repeated"—embodies the passionate hope of the human race. The appeal of Hiroshima . . . has nothing to do with politics. When foreigners come to Hiroshima, you often hear them say, "The politicians of the world should come to Hiroshima and contemplate the world's political problems on their knees before this Cenotaph."

ON *May 18, 1974, India conducted its first nuclear test.*

As the fortieth anniversary of the bombing approached, the Hiroshima peace center was nominally still in place—now in the Tanimoto home. Its principal project in the seventies had been to arrange a series of adoptions of orphans and abandoned Japanese babies, who had nothing particularly to do with the atomic bomb. The adoptive parents were in Hawaii and the mainland United States. Tanimoto had made three more speaking trips, in the mainland States in 1976 and 1982, and in Hawaii in 1981. He had retired from his pulpit in 1982.

Kiyoshi Tanimoto was over seventy now. The average age of all hibakusha was sixty-two. The surviving hibakusha had been polled by *Chugoku Shimbun* in 1984, and 54.3 per cent of them said they thought that nuclear weapons would be used again. Tanimoto read in the papers that the United States and the Soviet Union were steadily climbing the steep steps of deterrence. He and Chisa both drew health-maintenance allowances as hibakusha, and he had a modest pension from the United Church of Japan. He lived in a snug little house with a radio and two television sets, a washing machine, an electric oven, and a refrigerator, and he had a compact Mazda automobile, manufactured in Hiroshima. He ate too much. He got up at six every morning and took an hour's walk with his small woolly dog, Chiko. He was slowing down a bit. His memory, like the world's, was getting spotty.

READ MORE IN PENGUIN

In every corner of the world, on every subject under the sun, Penguin represents quality and variety – the very best in publishing today.

For complete information about books available from Penguin – including Puffins, Penguin Classics and Arkana – and how to order them, write to us at the appropriate address below. Please note that for copyright reasons the selection of books varies from country to country.

In the United Kingdom: Please write to *Dept. EP, Penguin Books Ltd, Bath Road, Harmondsworth, West Drayton, Middlesex UB7 0DA*

In the United States: Please write to *Consumer Services, Penguin Putnam Inc., 405 Murray Hill Parkway, East Rutherford, New Jersey 07073-2136.* VISA and MasterCard holders call 1-800-631-8571 to order Penguin titles

In Canada: Please write to *Penguin Books Canada Ltd, 10 Alcorn Avenue, Suite 300, Toronto, Ontario M4V 3B2*

In Australia: Please write to *Penguin Books Australia Ltd, 487 Maroondah Highway, Ringwood, Victoria 3134*

In New Zealand: Please write to *Penguin Books (NZ) Ltd, Private Bag 102902, North Shore Mail Centre, Auckland 10*

In India: Please write to *Penguin Books India Pvt Ltd, 11 Community Centre, Panchsheel Park, New Delhi 110017*

In the Netherlands: Please write to *Penguin Books Netherlands bv, Postbus 3507, NL-1001 AH Amsterdam*

In Germany: Please write to *Penguin Books Deutschland GmbH, Metzlerstrasse 26, 60594 Frankfurt am Main*

In Spain: Please write to *Penguin Books S. A., Bravo Murillo 19, 1°B, 28015 Madrid*

In Italy: Please write to *Penguin Italia s.r.l., Via Vittòrio Emanuele 45/a, 20094 Corsico, Milano*

In France: Please write to *Penguin France, 12, Rue Prosper Ferradou, 31700 Blagnac*

In Japan: Please write to *Penguin Books Japan Ltd, Iidabashi KM-Bldg, 2-23-9 Koraku, Bunkyo-Ku, Tokyo 112-0004*

In South Africa: Please write to *Penguin Books South Africa (Pty) Ltd, P.O. Box 751093, Gardenview, 2047 Johannesburg*

READ MORE IN PENGUIN

Published or forthcoming:

Ulysses   James Joyce

Written over a seven-year period, from 1914 to 1921, *Ulysses* has survived bowdlerization, legal action and bitter controversy. An undisputed modernist classic, its ceaseless verbal inventiveness and astonishingly wide-ranging allusions confirm its standing as an imperishable monument to the human condition. 'Everybody knows now that *Ulysses* is the greatest novel of the century'   Anthony Burgess, *Observer*

Nineteen Eighty-Four   George Orwell

Hidden away in the Record Department of the Ministry of Truth, Winston Smith skilfully rewrites the past to suit the needs of the Party. Yet he inwardly rebels against the totalitarian world he lives in, which controls him through the all-seeing eye of Big Brother. 'His final masterpiece ... *Nineteen Eighty-Four* is enthralling' Timothy Garton Ash, *New York Review of Books*

The Day of the Locust *and* **The Dream Life of Balso Snell**
Nathanael West

These two novellas demonstrate the fragility of the American dream. In *The Day of the Locust*, talented young artist Todd Hackett has been brought to Hollywood to work in a major studio. He discovers a surreal world of tarnished dreams, where violence and hysteria lurk behind the glittering façade. 'The best of the Hollywood novels, a nightmare vision of humanity destroyed by its obsession with film' J. G. Ballard, *Sunday Times*

The Myth of Sisyphus   Albert Camus

The Myth of Sisyphus is one of the most profound philosophical statements written this century. It is a discussion of the central idea of absurdity that Camus was to develop in his novel *The Outsider*. Here Camus poses the fundamental question – Is life worth living? – and movingly argues for an acceptance of reality that encompasses revolt, passion and, above all, liberty.